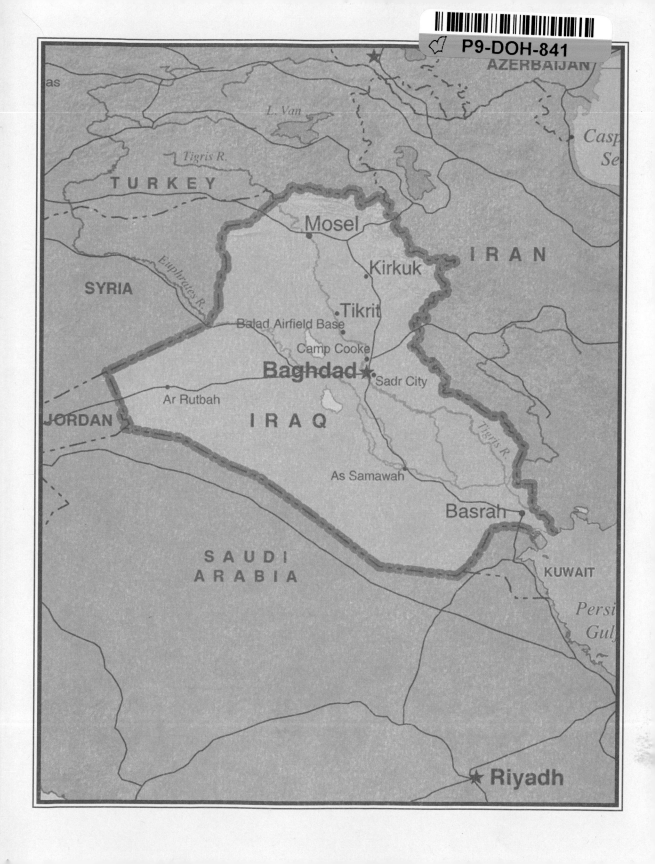

FAITH *in the* SERVICE

FAITH
in the
SERVICE

INSPIRATIONAL STORIES FROM LDS SERVICEMEN AND SERVICEWOMEN

COMPILED AND ILLUSTRATED BY
CHAD S. HAWKINS

FOREWORD BY
GENERAL BRUCE CARLSON

DESERET
BOOK

SALT LAKE CITY, UTAH

If you would like to share personal military experiences with the author for a future publication, you may contact him:

Chad Hawkins
P. O. Box 292
Layton, UT 84041
artist@integrity.com
www.chadhawkins.com

Text and pen-and-ink illustrations © 2008 Chad Hawkins Art, Inc.

Library of Congress Cataloging-in-Publication Data

Hawkins, Chad S., 1971–
   Faith in the service : inspirational stories from Latter-day Saint servicemen and servicewomen / compiled and illustrated by Chad S. Hawkins.
     p.   cm.
   ISBN 978-1-59038-905-8 (hardcover : alk. paper)
   1. Mormons—Religious life. 2. Soldiers—Religious life. I. Title.
   BX8656.H39 2008
   289.3092'273—dc22
   [B]   2008004663

Printed in the United States of America
R. R. Donnelley and Sons, Crawfordsville, IN

10 9 8 7 6 5 4 3 2 1

To my father, Lt. Col. Spencer E. Hawkins (Army),
Vietnam veteran (Ret.)

CONTENTS

CONTENTS

LIVING THE GOSPEL IN DESERT FATIGUES

CHAPLAINS IN THE SERVICE

CONTENTS

ACKNOWLEDGMENTS

As I began this project, I was not prepared for the overwhelming support I was about to receive. This support of others is what made this book possible and is a testament to its mission.

Gene Wikle and Michael Haller: At the conclusion of my stay with you in Kabul, Afghanistan, we were all driving to the airport for my departure. I thanked you for your kindness and support and you both shared the same supportive sentiment: "We are part of your team. We are doing this for the cause of this project." During our brief time together, you both opened my eyes to many lessons of life.

The faithful Saints serving at Camp Eggers: I love you. Partaking of your spirit is something I will never forget. Thank you for investing a little of yourselves in this book and showing me such love and kindness.

Chaplain Erik Harp: You are a spiritual giant and are blessing the lives of thousands. Thank you for providing Christlike service to our beloved troops. I am grateful for your friendship and example.

General Bruce Carlson: Thank you for taking the time to share your insights and for strengthening this project. It was a pleasure to work with you. I am grateful for the many years you have served our nation in the military.

Frank Clawson and Richard Whaley (Church Military Relations Division): Thank you for your direction and for building the kingdom by serving our members in the military.

FOREWORD

General Bruce Carlson
U.S. Air Force

Once again this nation finds itself at war. Young men, and now even more young women, are deploying to faraway locations where they are fighting to preserve our safety and security and establish freedom and democracy in depressed lands. War of any degree of severity is the most devastating, crippling, and horrific of events. That war is visiting our generation should be no surprise to Latter-day Saints. Moroni, speaking directly to us and of our time, predicted "wars [and] rumors of wars" (Mormon 8:30). When the Savior instructed the Prophet Joseph, He informed him that in this very dispensation "the whole earth shall be in commotion" (D&C 45:26).

We have been chosen to live out our mortality on this earth during these troubling times, and one measure of our success and progress in this life will be the amount and quality of service we render to those we share this space with. It is easy to be discouraged, even depressed, at times like these, when war and commotion are the order of the day. However, we have been promised that as we lose ourselves in service to others we will soon forget our own burdens and see beyond the cares of the day to a more long-lasting view of life, one that is much more satisfying and much more rewarding, even a view of life eternal.

General Carlson was commissioned in 1971 and has been awarded the Legion of Merit, Air Force Commendation Medal, and Air Force Achievement Medal.

In one of the greatest sermons ever preached, King Benjamin advised his people of this great principle when he told them that when they were in the service of their fellow man they were actually in direct service of their God. Understanding the power of this principle allows us to see the great opportunity that noble service affords each of us. Righteous and selfless service unlocks the keys of heaven and allows us to feel a small part of what the Savior felt as he walked the plains of Judea and the shores of Galilee, searching for those who would listen to his message and accept his service on their behalf.

Included in this book is a remarkable record of unselfish service in our time. Dedicated men and women, many of them in our armed forces, who have given their lives in service to their nation and their fellow man, will tell you, mostly in their own words, of the Lord's blessings as they have followed his direction to be about the business of service. You will be moved to action as you read of their uplifting and life-changing opportunities to serve. That this may assist you to be more sensitive to those around you who are in need of such service is my prayer.

INTRODUCTION

I buckled myself in, knowing I was embarking on a trip of a lifetime. My two-hour flight from Dubai, United Arab Emirates, to Kabul, Afghanistan, transported me from a growing city of extreme wealth, fashion, and opulence to a war-torn land stricken with third-world poverty. Prior to my flight, I made an effort to procure a window seat because I knew I would want to look out and absorb the view during the entire journey. After leaving the Arabian Peninsula and the Persian Gulf, our plane initially directed us over Iran and then Afghanistan. Small villages began to appear, providing new meaning to the word *isolated*. Without any trace of road or trail, these clusters of humanity were islands unto themselves. The topography consisted of deserts and jagged mountains, which dominated the landscape by turns. Although it was hard to believe that water ever relieved this scorched land, the evidence could be seen in a network of dried river beds and barren lakes. The only color we could see consisted of variations of umber brown.

As I studied this land reminiscent of a brown lunar landscape, my mind pondered this ancient and historically volatile region. Archaeological evidence supports the idea that this area had some of the world's earliest human inhabitants. The vast time line of tribal civilizations here were conquered by a host of people, including the Persians, Alexander the Great, the Arabs and

Turks, and Genghis Khan, to name a few. In recent times, occupiers have included the British, decades of tyrannical reign under the Soviets, and the Taliban. With great anticipation, I looked forward to arriving in Afghanistan and seeing with my own eyes a rebuilding civilization that has endured more than words can describe.

Within minutes of being picked up at the Kabul International Airport, I was fitted with a level-three armored vest and taken to see a crater on the perimeter of the airport. The cavity and surrounding destruction were created only sixteen days earlier by a suicide bomber who detonated his explosive-laden vehicle. Gene Wikle and Michael Haller (both of whom are now dear friends) were my escorts during my stay in Afghanistan. They were anxious to provide me with vital information and orientation details. To be honest, I really did not hear much of what they were saying during my first exposure to the land. I was more concerned about the white-knuckle, ban-zai approach to driving on the streets of Kabul. Laws governing the movement of traffic do not seem to exist in *any* form. The person with nerves of steel and with the least regard for the condition of his vehicle is the one who advances. Among the moving maze of vehicles, donkeys, bicycles, and hand-pulled wagons were children, in harm's way, pleading for donations.

I arrived at my hotel near dusk. I first passed a set of security guards armed with AK–47s, a security-check ritual reminiscent of an airport security screening. As grateful as I was to have a security presence surrounding the hotel, it did not necessarily put my mind at ease. Knowing my hotel needed security was of itself a cause for concern. Once in my room, I locked the door and flipped on the television, not knowing what to expect. To my surprise (and it *was* a surprise), I found a few familiar channels, including ESPN. After watching the recap of the day's college football games and reconnecting with my love of sports, I began to feel like this was just another stay in a hotel. Then the hotel's power went out, the room went black, and

As the author made his way through a maze of old Russian military fortifications on a hill overlooking Afghanistan's capital city, he made friends with several curious children.

I heard an explosion in the distance—and I was reminded that this was not going to be just another hotel visit.

I spent the majority of my time in the nation's capital city on Camp Eggers. This U.S. military base is located near the U.S. embassy and Afghanistan's presidential palace. The security precautions to enter Camp Eggers were awesome to witness. A labyrinth of high bunker walls with strategically placed armed guards ensured that only the authorized could enter. Although I was still on Afghan soil, being on the American compound surrounded by military personnel gave me a sense of being in the States. Upon entering the camp, I had some of the same patriotic feeling I get *every time* I return to the United States after traveling abroad. To show my blue passport and be welcomed onto the base was for me an honor and privilege.

One day, I spent long hours on the base conducting interviews, writing this book, and being introduced to key military personnel. It had been a successful and wonderful day. The sun was setting, and it was time for me to be escorted off the base and back to my hotel. As I exited the fortified, high walls and made my first step onto the streets of Kabul, I had an immediate and powerful impression. I have the same feeling every time I leave the temple. My wife and I typically attend the Bountiful Temple in Utah. Those who have visited this temple know of its beautiful setting. It has a steep mountainside directly to the east and views overlooking the Great Salt Lake to the west. Despite this natural grandeur, every time I leave the temple I have a significant sense of leaving the celestial and entering the temporal—leaving spiritual safety and entering spiritual uncertainty. The moment I left the security of the military base, I was placed in a very real position of physical danger—leaving physical safety and entering physical uncertainty. I thought of how President Gordon B. Hinckley referred to temples in a dedicatory prayer as "a shelter of peace from the noise and clamor of the world, a refuge in time of distress, a sanctuary" (Baton Rouge Louisiana Temple dedicatory prayer). This observation reminded me how truly important temples are and how blessed we are to have access to the temple, our base of spiritual safety.

The spiritual highlight of my time in Afghanistan was certainly the two-hour church service with the Saints. In the Islamic faith, Friday is the holy day, and therefore the soldiers serving in the country usually get the day off. To accommodate this schedule, LDS church services are also organized on Friday. The room set aside as the chapel was equipped to serve several denominations. To the side of the room were instruments prepared for a gospel jam session. I saw guitars, amps, a drum set, and a keyboard. For our service, we just used the keyboard. Gathered were twenty-seven Saints, consisting mostly of soldiers, with a few civilians (contractors, U.S. embassy staff, Kabul University professors). For me, it was an emotionally powerful experience from the very beginning. The invocation included a humble petition to Heavenly Father for the safety and well-being of "our families back home." The prayer also included such specific words and phrases as "school," "choose the right," "good friends," "not to be lonely," and "that they may feel our love." I have never heard a prayer that united those present as much as this one did. I immediately thought of the church meetings in my home ward. There, the group prayers consistently include petitions to protect those at war and in harm's way. It was an interesting perspective to be among those who were "at war and in harm's way" and to hear them pray for their loved ones back home.

The first meeting combined priesthood brethren with the Relief Society sisters. Sister Kristine Stoehner took a few minutes and shared a very appropriate Relief Society message. As she concluded, I witnessed how the tradition of meaningful Relief Society handouts was alive and well, even in Afghanistan. With a war-zone touch, she demonstrated great resourcefulness by passing around handouts in her Kevlar soldier's helmet. I then was privileged to share a message based on President Howard W. Hunter's invitation to make the temple the "great symbol of our membership." We discussed how the temple can be a strength and comfort, even when we are deployed at war. For me, however, the most important part of my message was at the end, when I told those present how I loved them and thanked them in behalf of all those back home for serving our country.

The Spirit continued with us into sacrament meeting. It was a powerful sight to see worthy priesthood holders, wearing their desert fatigues and sidearms, bless and pass the sacrament. Only one man in the room was wearing a formal suit. The faith of those present invited the loving comfort of the Spirit. Being among these faithful Saints was a powerful example of how Zion is indeed "the pure in heart" (D&C 97:21). Zion is wherever righteous Saints gather. In closing, we sang "God Be with You till We Meet Again," which was for me very significant. I will always be grateful to have been so blessed as to have experienced such a gentle, yet significant event.

After accomplishing my tasks in Kabul, Afghanistan, I departed and flew to Frankfurt, Germany. After a series of extended layovers and distant flights, I arrived in Germany at 6:00 o'clock Sunday morning. I drove straight from

Left to right: Brothers in the gospel, Ian Hoag, Chad Hawkins, and Rob Horner, at Camp Eggers, Kabul, Afghanistan

the airport to Kaiserslautern, where I arrived in time to attend both an American servicemen's ward and a German branch. The city of Kaiserslautern and the chapel there are of great sentimental importance to me. My father, Spencer E. Hawkins, served in the army, and my family was stationed in the area twice. Later, I was called to serve my full-time mission to Frankfurt, Germany. As a missionary, I had the opportunity to serve in Kaiserslautern for six months. Therefore, I felt right at home in the city, and worshipping in that chapel again brought back many beloved memories from my mission.

Since the Kaiserslautern area has a huge American military presence, my purpose for visiting the area was to meet with many Church members who had war experience "downrange." The majority of my time was spent at the nearby Landstuhl Regional Medical Center (LRMC). The LRMC is the largest military hospital outside of the continental United States. It serves as the nearest treatment center for wounded soldiers coming from Iraq and Afghanistan. The hospital has additional significance to me personally because it is the place of my birth. My escort onto the massive facility was LDS Chaplain Erik Harp. Among his many vital responsibilities, he serves as the hospital's intensive care unit (ICU) chaplain. He lovingly refers to the patients and the staff of the ICU as his flock and ministry. I spent some time with him in the ICU and was introduced to the staff. I was briefed on the medical condition of many of the warriors who lay unconscious. Although we were not in the war zone, the destruction of war literally lay before my eyes. Filling the beds were Romanian soldiers who had been taken out by an improvised explosive device (IED). Burns covered nearly 30 percent of their bodies. A Romanian physician was present to assist with translation and aid in their treatment. I was privileged to be allowed to simply stand back and observe.

Later in the afternoon an announcement requesting "manpower at the ER" was made over the hospital's broadcast system. Chaplain Harp stopped what he was doing and said, "Chad come with me. You have to see this." We walked directly to the outdoor receiving area for the hospital's emergency room, where nearly fifty hospital workers were already assembled. A military plane carrying wounded warriors had recently arrived at the nearby Ramstein Air Force Base. Buses transporting those wounded in the war on terror were on their way to the hospital. The system was an impressive example of efficiency. The journey from Iraq to the hospital required less than seven hours. The incredibly quick transportation can add shock to the soldiers' awareness, considering the stark contrast of environment. Two buses arrived simultaneously. All present organized themselves into well-rehearsed positions. One by one, soldiers were taken off the buses and placed on gurneys. The moment the soldiers were lowered onto their gurneys, a chaplain was speaking to them, telling them they had safely arrived at the Landstuhl Hospital and thanking them for their service. I had the privilege of escorting a female soldier on her gurney up to her hospital room. Along the way she remained somber and oblivious to all around her. As we pushed her down the hallway she said, "I just want them to fix me up so I can go back. I just want them to fix me up so I can go back. I have got to get back." She spoke with a clenched jaw, while focusing on the ceiling above. She uttered her thoughts so quietly that I sensed the words were not for us to hear. Her deep desire to persevere and fulfill her duty was an inspiration to witness.

Due to its visibly important responsibility to our nation's military, the Landstuhl Regional Medical Center receives a great amount of attention. During my several-day visit I was introduced to U.S. ambassadors, foreign secretaries of defense, and six U.S. Congressmen. I was able to observe members of the German media as they did live interviews for an upcoming radio news production. On several occasions I noted how some members of the military view the media with negative skepticism. I experienced this in a significant and personal way while being introduced to one of the hospital's physicians. The doctor's warm greeting and handshake quickly changed once I was introduced as "Chad Hawkins, who is here doing interviews for an upcoming book." At that moment, the doctor withdrew his hand and walked away without another word. I was stunned at his instantaneous change of demeanor. I was then informed that many in the military refuse to have anything to do with the media due to their perception of the media's anti-military reporting. From then on, I asked to be introduced simply as, "Chad Hawkins." (At this moment, as I am writing this in the Landstuhl Hospital, Brahms' Lullaby is being played over the hospital's loudspeaker. See the story titled "Brahms' Lullaby" to learn why that is so significant.)

The origin of this book comes from an experience I had at the Salt Lake International Airport, as I was returning from the Sacramento California Temple open house. After deboarding the plane, I proceeded toward the baggage claim. As I moved down the escalator, I noticed well over one hundred people looking up at me with flags, handmade signs, and dozens of yellow balloons. I quickly realized this welcome-home crowd was not for me. Due to the sense of heightened anticipation, I could tell a momentous reunion was about to take place. As I worked through the huddled mass I heard, "There he is!" Behind me, a soldier dressed in desert fatigues began to make his way down the escalator. On cue, a men's a cappella choir began singing "The Star-Spangled Banner." Despite being in a bustling airport where hundreds of travelers were focused on their own cares, the vast room became quiet. *All* present showed respect for their national anthem and the coming home of a soldier. Hats were removed and hands were placed over hearts. During the singing of our nation's hymn, the soldier was embracing his children and kissing his wife. As the anthem concluded, everyone present roared with applause while wiping away their tears. It was a powerful moment that united all present. The spirit of the extraordinary moment continued when the choir's repertoire seamlessly blended into the singing of "Love at Home." What a gift it was to witness this powerful moment depicting the love of God, family, and country.

Not long after that experience, I was following my normal routine of weekend yard work when I noticed my dear neighbor and her sons working in their yard. I then remembered why her husband was not there working with them. He had recently been deployed to Iraq. Their capable ability to take care of items back home while their husband and father serves our

The author meets with the Kabul LDS Servicemen's Group in September 2007.

country remains an inspiration to me. I realized that both those deployed and those back home who support them have stories to tell that will bless the lives of others. This book contains some of these stories.

Meeting with and interviewing members of the Church for this publication has been an honor and a blessing. I was fortunate to meet and spend time with most of those featured in this book. During these conversations, several shared how discussing their experiences with me had been therapeutic. Telling the stories, or "journaling" them, enabled some to work through experiences and appreciate them for what they were. In many cases, they had not formalized their thoughts or shared them with anyone before. While pondering their experiences, some shared how their testimonies had grown by taking the time to recognize the Lord's hand in their lives.

Often during these interviews, those with whom I met wore desert fatigues, body armor, and sidearms. Despite their intimidating outward appearance, many openly shared emotion. Voices cracked, tears were wiped away, and lengthy pauses often accompanied their sincere thoughts. Their tender emotions defied the stereotype of a hardened military soldier. One such experience occurred when I asked a brother if the temple had strengthened him during his deployment. As his thoughts went to his wife and the temple, his emotions left him unable to speak.

The stories featured in this book remain largely in the words of the individual, with only minor editing. I hope readers will sense the tender feelings mingled within each story. I am grateful to those who were willing to share their personal experiences, insights, and testimonies. Everyone did so with the utmost humility and honorable motives. Their submissions are further enhanced by their own photography. Wishing each story to be as credible and as accurate as possible, I invited each person to review his or her story for accuracy. You will see that deployment dates are given with each story. Please note that these dates were current at the time of my interview with each individual; but certainly the passage of time and new assignments will change dates and places of service.

It is important to recognize the support given to this project by *all* involved. From the beginning, assistance was offered me by Church members serving in harm's way. An example of this support comes from Brother Gene Wikle, who serves as senior group leader in Afghanistan. (Group leader is an ecclesiastical position unique to certain areas where the United States military is deployed. The senior group leader in an area supervises many other group leaders and reports to an area presidency.) He wrote me the following:

Chad,

Those serving in these war-torn countries are all latter-day pioneers. Members of the Church serving in Iraq and Afghanistan have a special mission to be pioneers, providing beacons of hope, freedom, and a better life for the good people of Iraq and Afghanistan. As we share our stories and testimonies with you, you serve as a pioneer for us. You have the opportunity to tell our story. On behalf of all the members of the Church serving in Afghanistan, thank you! We appreciate all you are doing for us.

Best regards,
Gene Wikle

Brother Michael Haller wrote, "Thank you so very much for gathering these stories. They are important and need the light of day thrust upon them. I know it with all my heart."

Brother Derek Hable said in an interview, "Thank you for following your impression to write this book. It means a lot to us that you would be willing to travel to this part of the world and tell about the Lord's kingdom in Afghanistan."

Receiving these kind words of encouragement has been a humble motivation for me. Many unsolicited handwritten notes supporting this effort were also presented to me.

These Church members in uniform have a solid understanding of their military objective and are diligent about fulfilling their individual duty. What makes these members special is how they additionally recognize the Lord's objective and have a sense that they are aiding his cause. They have a broad understanding of the world around them and feel honored to be a part of the work preceding the Savior's second coming. One brother volunteered, "I do not think what I am doing over here is heroic. I am just doing what needs to be done. If I do not make it home, I know my sacrifice will not be in vain. The soldiers I know feel the same way. We are just doing our part in our corner of the war to improve the lives of Iraqis by creating an environment where they can live, grow, and prosper. We are building a foundation upon which personal and national liberty can be built. By so doing, we will earn their trust, and they will open their minds to the new ideas that will accompany their freedom." Although Church members serving in the military do not preach the gospel in Iraq or Afghanistan, they still spread the gospel by creating an environment of democracy where the gospel will one day take root and flourish. They do not proselytize; rather, they focus on their duty. As they live the gospel according to their conscience, they know the gospel of Jesus Christ will take care of itself.

While in Kabul, Afghanistan, I had the opportunity to hike with others to the top of a prominent hill located in the middle of the city. From the hill's apex, I could look though the early morning haze and envision scenes of tragic history, current struggle, and a promising future. It was not long before our group was noticed by a cluster of children who were flying a colorful kite. One by one, the children made their way closer to take a look at us. Their energy and innocence are universal to all children, regardless of nationality or economic circumstance. I shared with them the mints in my camera bag and felt like I was making friends for life. They then ran to entertain us by playing on their "playground." I watched in awe as these kids climbed on the remnants of rusty Russian military equipment the same way my children climb on jungle gyms at our neighborhood park. As my group waved good-bye to these precious little ones, one of my companions said, "Hopefully, their generation will be the one to which the restored gospel will be preached." That thought made an impact on me. Before descending the hill, I looked at my newfound friends and prayed that his sentiment would come true.

This experience on the hill is among several once-in-a-lifetime moments I had within a relatively short time. I looked into an orphan's eyes and saw hope. I shook a soldier's hand and felt purpose. I observed a chaplain and saw charity. I met with a family missing a deployed father and sensed support. I assisted a wounded warrior and knew his valor. I was among humanitarians and witnessed Christlike service. One cannot be among such amazing people and not be motivated to take a little less and give a little more.

Having grown up in a military family, I have early recollections of my father remembering the military in his prayers. Even at a young age, I was taught by example to pray for the safety of those in uniform, both during times of peace and war. Believing in the example my father set for me, I have always made an effort to raise my family to regularly remember the military in our thoughts and prayers. Associating and praying with many who are featured in this book has prompted me to give more effort and sincerity to my prayers. Following their example, I have learned to also pray for the families of those in the military and that the soldiers may achieve their objective.

Being among the Saints downrange in the war zone was an incredibly powerful experience. I expected to learn about how hard it is to maintain high LDS standards in such a severe environment. In most cases I found the opposite to be true. One brother said, "I feel like there is a continuous flow of the Spirit here. It is as if I am plugged into the Spirit like when I was a full-time missionary. The Spirit will never leave me, although I can leave Him through disobedience."

I encourage the readers of this book to be like the faithful Latter-day Saints who choose to remain faithful while serving in the harshest of circumstances. Never put your membership "on hold"; instead, choose to spiritually grow in your life today. If our brothers and sisters can flourish in a dangerous physical and spiritual environment, how much should we be able to progress when we are in safety back home? Wherever we find ourselves, we can live in the world and not be of the world. This dedication to living the gospel was firmly stated by First Lieutenant David DeMille: "There is no compromising when it comes to keeping the commandments. There is not a different gospel in a combat zone. . . . It is all the same. Regardless of where you are, there are no excuses." His commitment and mature understanding of the gospel can be an inspiration to us all.

This book features multiple examples of Church members seeing a need and then creating a way to accomplish noble acts of service. If we back home were to make an effort to step outside of our own comfortable routine, how many ways could we discover to ease the burdens of someone in need? While in the war zone, Master Sergeant John Gardner told me, "I do not know if I will be so fortunate as to make it through another day. I know every day is a gift. It's like my father used to say, 'One thing is for sure—no one gets out of this life alive.' Therefore, I try to make the most of each opportunity to serve and grow."

Our common freedoms are not so common. The high quality of life we enjoy in the United States is the extreme *exception*, not the norm. Jesus Christ is the author of our freedom. Whether we are fighting the battle against terror or struggling with our own personal battles, the gospel of Jesus Christ can provide safety and an assured victory. May the lessons our brothers and sisters learn in the battlefield be of great strength to us as we apply them to our lives back home.

This book details several worthwhile causes. As I met the people involved and personally witnessed them accomplishing so much with so little, I had a desire to do my part to further their charitable efforts. Read their stories in this book, and then take a few moments to visit their websites and learn how you can participate. I include the following information with their permission:

The Afghanistan Orphanage Project (see "Persistence, Miracles, and Eternal Relationships")
Layne S. Pace, President
1021 N. 500 W.
Orem, Utah 84057
(801) 376–5000
Email: Layne@taoproject.org
Website: www.taoproject.org

Women of Hope Project (see "Toy Animals, Stuffed Hot Water Bottles, and Love")
Kristine Stoehner
9321 Nettleton Drive
Anchorage, Alaska 99507
Email: jstoehne@aol.com
Website: www.womenofhopeproject.org

Events DOWNRANGE

We live in a time of wars and rumors of wars.
Many Church members have personally felt the effects of war, and
many more will likely participate in these conflicts. We are grateful
for the personal sacrifices they and their families have made in
defense of freedom and liberty. Especially during these challenging
times, we want them to know of our love and heartfelt thanks
for their courageous and devoted service.

—Frank W. Clawson, LDS Church Director of Military Relations

DELIVERING JOY IN A BLACKHAWK

Chief Warrant Officer 2 Jared Kimber
U.S. Army, Blackhawk Pilot
Iraq, three deployments

While serving in Kirkuk, Iraq, my living quarters were on the edge of our base. I lived so close to the perimeter that I could see through the wire and watch the Iraqi children on the outside. The children frequently occupied their time by playing games. These kids did not have anything. I never saw them play with any kind of toy. Yet they were able to find joy by playing tag or games of soccer in their bare feet using an old can instead of a ball. My flying partner had children back home, so he was very sensitive to the needs of these kids. Together we watched the children make the best of their situation.

One day as the children played, my partner and I walked over to the fence and threw a few toys over the tall barrier. The kids were very excited for the gifts and amazed that anyone would give them toys.

We shared with our friends on base what we had done, along with the touching reaction of the children. The word of our experience began to spread. It was not long before we were approached by authorities in the air force. They explained that the military had been working to improve U.S. relations with a strategic small town. The military had gone to great lengths to foster and maintain a high level of public support among those living in the village. We were asked to assist with this objective by gathering and

Iraqi children wearing new clothes and holding their precious toys

delivering toys in our Blackhawk to the children living there. I loved the idea because I knew it would bless and bring joy to the lives of children living in desperate circumstances. We gathered toys by spreading word of our project on base and also back home. Our families back in the States collected toys in creative ways and then sent them to us.

After only a few weeks we were ready to go on our first "toy bombing" mission. A team of special forces was first sent to secure a location in the town. A translator was among the first on the scene to inform locals what was about to transpire. We circled up above until everyone on the ground was in position and we were cleared to land. I then landed my helicopter into the secured zone. It was wonderful to watch the children's expressions as I unloaded the cargo with my crew.

We had every kind of toy you could imagine—Frisbees, stuffed animals, soccer balls, and footballs—along with some clothes and shoes. We were allowed to play with the kids for about thirty minutes. They knew what to do with soccer balls, but we had to show them how to catch and throw the footballs. The best part of our mission was taking a few minutes to play with them. The kids had a great time. The parents told us through translators how much they appreciated us thinking of their children.

This first "toy drop" was a huge success, and we continued to get shipments of toys from back home. I guess word spread, and loving people back in the States continued to send us toys. Shipments came in "from sea to shining sea." The toys filled our building and hallways. It seemed that we could not deliver them fast enough to keep up with the toys coming in. Depending on our mission, we would sometimes fly low and drop the toys without landing. We were able to do this in several villages throughout Iraq. It was not long before we noticed a difference. Before, when we had flown over towns, people would run indoors and hide. Now, however, the villagers would come out and greet us with waves, even when we did not have anything to give. I know we made a difference in building trusting relationships.

It was a great feeling to give something to children who actually appreciated the gift. Kids back home have so much that many of them do not appreciate what they have. As a father of a one-year-old girl, I am grateful beyond belief that I can provide for her when so many children go without.

Grateful Iraqi youths wave good-bye to the generous Americans who brought them such joy and hope.

LISTEN THE *FIRST* TIME

Chief Warrant Officer 2 Jared Kimber
U.S. Army, Blackhawk Pilot
Iraq, three deployments

During my second deployment to Iraq, we were stationed in Kirkuk. As pilots of medical-evacuation helicopters, we have to be ready to pick up wounded soldiers and bring them to the hospital at any hour of the day or night. When soldiers suffer injuries, we are the first ones they call.

One night we got the call to rescue some soldiers who were shot up pretty bad. It is always better to not be seen when flying in a hostile environment—if the enemy can see us, they can shoot a missile at us, and so we take every precaution to be as stealthy as possible. We flew this nighttime mission blacked out (without any lights on). Our night-vision goggles enabled us to navigate at night.

As we approached the area where we were to make our pickup, I tried to make radio contact with the soldiers. But as I diverted my attention down to the radio I felt I should look up instead. I knew I needed to make radio contact, so I continued focusing on the radio. Again I was prompted to look up. I still ignored the prompting. Suddenly it was as if someone grabbed my helmet and forced me to look up. I looked and saw the silhouette of one of our blacked-out helicopters flying near us. I instinctively knew that the oncoming helicopter was flying in a pair, and I immediately looked for the second

Chief Warrant Officer 2 Jared Kimber pilots a Blackhawk helicopter.

helicopter. At the same time, I yelled to my copilot to turn left. Instead, he dove the helicopter downward. As we dove our aircraft, I looked to my left just in time to see the second helicopter upon us and flaring upward.

I still do not know how we missed each other. It all happened instantaneously. I guess the second helicopter saw us the same time we saw it, because it was climbing when we were diving and we somehow avoided a collision. We were so close that when I looked out my window I could see the two pilots in their seats! It was a very scary experience. If I had looked out my window half a second later, we would have collided for sure.

I have since thought many times about that experience. If I had looked out after the first prompting, it would not have been a close call and we could have maneuvered easily out of each other's way. I ignored the Spirit twice; thankfully Heavenly Father was not going to let me ignore it a third time. I learned from this experience that I need to stop being stubborn and pay attention to the promptings of the Spirit the *first* time. I know that Heavenly Father is looking out for me, and I need to do my part to let him take care of me.

I NOW KNOW WHY I AM HERE

First Lieutenant Michael Beggs

U.S. Army, 831st LNO/DOD Transportation Liaison, U.S. Embassy Kabul, Afghanistan, October 2006–January 2008

I first involved myself with the kids at Bagram, Afghanistan, when I saw them working at the gate of our military post. The kids were paid to keep the secured gate area tidy and free of trash. I'd been deployed in Kuwait and Afghanistan for about ten months, and I'd started to really pine for my wife and one-year-old son. My son had been born after I mobilized, so I had only about five weeks with him. Therefore, I was always happy to see the kids on the base. I made an effort to learn more about them, earned their trust, and began working with them.

Being around the kids was a huge morale boost. All of them were third-world poor and had suffered greatly under the Taliban's oppression. Yet they still managed to stay positive and be thankful for what they did have. Some of them had lost their fathers and brothers to the Taliban, and none of the girls were allowed to attend school. I was amazed to see that even though they had so little, they still managed to look out for other kids who had even less. The older kids would always make sure to let me know which children were the worst off and needed the most help. Also, even though they had little themselves, they always found a way to share gifts with us to express their gratitude. They would share crafts and scarves. One gave jewelry for my

Lieutenant Beggs assists children with their job to keep the area clear of trash and debris.

wife made out of plastic and kite string. Their generosity would shame most people I know.

Until I met those kids, it was hard for me to personalize the war. I hadn't seen a bad guy or been shot at. I had experienced rocket attacks and been near IED explosions, but it all felt rather detached, as no one I knew was ever injured. I now know why I am here. These children deserve what we take for granted: freedom, safety, the right to pursue an education, food, clothing, and just a chance to be a child. An eight-year old boy should not have to be the family breadwinner.

One particularly hot day I noticed that the littlest girl, Hakima, was pulling at her clothes because she was so uncomfortable. She wore winter clothes in the summer because she had little else. It is common for the children to wear the same clothes for several days in a row. I decided to do something about it. I took her (and all of the little girls; they travel together for safety) to a store in the bazaar to buy her a lightweight summer dress. She was so happy it made me teary.

It then occurred to me that with the help of my family and friends, I could probably do a lot more. I sent out a blanket email to just about everyone I

Afghan boys modeling the clothes sent from Lieutenant Beggs's family

knew asking for donations. The response to my email was surprising. Folks who I thought would gladly send donations remained silent, while others sent packages immediately. The first package I received was filled with clothes from my wife, Kate; my mom, Darragh; and Sister Betts. They had gone out together shopping to purchase everything. I was proud of them, and I imagined them all together talking about what they would get.

When I distributed the clothes, the kids were so thankful! They were also clearly impressed that people would care enough to send them these precious items of clothing. The boys lined up and picked out one item each until everyone had something. Then they lined up again; each one of them was able to receive a couple of items that fit well. A few items still remained, and some of the boys sheepishly asked if they could have them for their siblings. Their humility and thoughtfulness was touching.

Girls and boys are the same around the world. Boys are perfectly happy as long as the clothing fits, while the girls were a little harder—their tastes were a bit more discerning. After finding something they liked, I had them go try them on to make sure they fit. After obtaining approval from the other girls, the deal was sealed. My family did a great job of finding clothes modest enough for the girls—no easy job in the United States.

I convinced them to model the clothes so I could send pictures to my family. After the first few photographs, the boys started to feel comfortable in front of the camera, and their delightful personalities started to show. One of the boys asked timidly if he could wear my military hat in a picture. After he wore it, all of the boys wanted a turn. They love pictures, and I was able to make prints and give them copies.

Hanging out with the kids in Afghanistan during my downtime has been the highlight of my deployment. I didn't help them as much as they helped me. Heavenly Father blessed me with the opportunity to meet them when I was feeling low. Spending time with them also helped me feel more connected to my family and friends back home. Many times I caught myself talking to the boys just as I did to my Boy Scouts in the Rock Hill Ward. Giving the gifts that my family sent to the girls reminded me of all of my little nieces and of how sweet and thoughtful my wife is. Serving others really lifted my spirits and helped me forget my own concerns.

I WAS PROMPTED WHAT TO SAY

First Sergeant David Fillmore
Utah Army National Guard
Iraq, 2003–2004

I was frequently given assignments to head patrols into insecure areas to accomplish a variety of well-defined missions. On many missions I was given the responsibility to provide security for specialists for their designated tasks. Our small caravans would consist of four to seven armored and unarmored vehicles. On one of these missions our task was to visit an old weapons factory, where the Iraqi government used to build and house weapons and missiles. We were escorting several chemical and weapons specialists. Along the way we made a series of wrong turns. By the time we realized we were in the wrong place, we were driving in a small village settlement. We turned the convoy around and headed to our intended destination.

After reaching our destination and accomplishing our goal, the specialists in our group mentioned that they had observed an unexploded missile half buried in the ground back near the small village. Knowing of the extreme danger of having such a powerful bomb near the community, we decided to go back and make plans for its removal. While we were at the village, I walked to a nearby shack to buy some cold sodas for our guys. Using broken English and sign language, the man who sold me the sodas asked what we were doing. After I told him about the dangerous bomb, the man responded by telling me of another unexploded bomb nearby. He explained that it was located in the median of one of Baghdad's major thoroughfares. Using his directions, we went to inspect this claim of a second unexploded bomb.

Once we arrived at the location, our first duty was to partially stop traffic and set up a secure perimeter. After the specialists verified that there was another bomb, they yelled at the people nearby, "Get back! Get back! Get away!" The bomb was a 152-millimeter artillery shell in the middle of the road, the largest in the Iraqi arsenal. The specialists were concerned that it might be a potential trap—a device that could be remote-

David Fillmore on patrol in Iraq

detonated. Our team was not prepared to disarm the artillery shell, and so we contacted our base to send out a squad equipped with a disarming robot.

While we waited, our mission evolved into keeping people away from the hazard. This became more difficult by the minute. The area was densely populated with pedestrians and an ever-increasing traffic jam. Although we left one lane open in each direction, impatient drivers began to drive wherever they could, hoping to make progress. Horns honked and tempers mounted.

After an hour, the team arrived to dispose of the bomb. Now that the bomb was being worked on, we were forced to completely close the road in all directions. By now, several hundred cars were backed up, and we were surrounded by at least a thousand people. Adding to the confusion, people were getting out of their cars and walking towards us. My team was thinned out and not properly prepared to deal with the escalating situation. The crowd repeatedly attempted to get closer than safety would allow, so I was consistently trying to back them up. There were only two other soldiers in my vicinity.

Then an Iraqi man came right up to me, pointed, and yelled in broken English, "You American! You shot my leg!" The man then showed me and the crowd his prosthetic leg. I tried to explain that I wasn't the one who shot him. He yelled again, "You American! You shot my leg!" As he said this, I could begin to sense the entire crowd becoming hostile. I remember thinking, *What are we going to do?* We had our machine guns locked and loaded. We took our weapons off safety, and I was considering my options. I seriously thought that this was going to be it—that if the mob didn't disperse once the guns opened up, I would be probably a dead person.

During this moment of tension, I remembered the words of the priesthood blessing I had received prior to leaving for Iraq. The blessing promised that I would return home safely. I thought, *But I do not want to live through this by shooting into this dense crowd.* Then the Spirit brought words into my mind telling me how I should respond to the man. Those words didn't make sense; they were provocative and it seemed they would only make things worse. But I was reminded of other times in my life when I needed to trust the Lord—and all had turned out well. When the man accused me again of shooting him, I said the words I was prompted to say: "Me no shoot you! Me no shoot leg!" I pointed to his leg. "Me shoot here!" I pointed to his heart.

The irate man then yelled, "You shoot in heart and in head!"

I responded firmly, "No. Me no shoot head! Me no shoot leg! Me shoot in heart!" I pointed to the heart.

The man responded, "But then I'm dead!"

I said, "Yes, if I shoot you, you are dead!" I pointed at the guy.

The man and the crowd became silent for several seconds. Then the man started to tell the crowd about the great American doctor who helped him with his injury and gave him his prosthetic leg. He praised the doctor and the nice people in the American hospital who cared for him. Instantly the mood of the crowd changed. The anger went away and everyone calmed down.

This lesson, among others in Iraq, taught me to trust in the Lord. For fear of provoking the crowd, I never would have responded to the angry man using those words if I had not been prompted by the Lord. I put my trust in Him and with His blessing the event had a peaceful conclusion.

BOMBING A MOTORCADE

Elder William K. Jackson*

U.S. Foreign Service, Regional Medical Officer
New Delhi, India, 2005

In 2005, I served as regional medical officer in the U.S. Foreign Service. I was stationed with my family in New Delhi, India. My responsibilities required me to travel throughout the region to neighboring countries, where I looked after the health and welfare of the official American community there. This travel often involved visiting Afghanistan, where many embassy-based Americans lived and worked.

I had an experience I will never forget during one of these Afghan visits. Early in the morning of Wednesday, November 16, 2005, I was leaving the city of Kandahar, in southern Afghanistan, in a convoy of six vehicles headed for the airport. Mine was an armored SUV, and the third car in line. The streets were crowed, as always, but the traffic was not as bad as sometimes. Just before we exited the city, a dark green sedan pulled out into the two-lane road and positioned itself in front of us, blocking our ability to pass and stay in tight formation. This was certainly not unusual in Kandahar traffic. The driver of our vehicle got right up on the sedan's bumper and hit his horn, succeeding in getting the sedan's driver to pull over a little and allow us to squeeze by. As we were driving past, the sedan swerved back toward us, and I knew that we were going to hit each other. I braced for the scrape of metal

16

Contorted metal is all that remained of Elder Jackson's vehicle. With the sedan in the position shown, he and the other passengers climbed out and ran to safety.

on metal. Instead, there was a deafening blast as the sedan driver detonated a car bomb while positioned on the right rear bumper of our car. Everything went dark—we were in the center of the explosion-cloud of smoke and dust—and it appeared to me that we were weightless for a moment. Our 11,000-plus pound vehicle was lifted into the air and thrown forty meters down the street, where we came to rest on our right side, facing back towards the site of the explosion. It all happened so fast that it was over before I realized what had occurred. Our car was on fire, with flames shooting up over the left side windows. Fortunately, somewhere between the explosion and our coming to a full stop, the thick, bulletproof front windshield had popped out, giving us an escape route from the burning vehicle. The four of us inside the car managed to crawl out and get across the road before, just seconds later, the fuel tank erupted in a second loud explosion and the vehicle was engulfed in flames.

The scene was a gruesome one, with smoke and fire and many local innocent casualties. It was not something I would ever want to witness again. The explosives had essentially atomized the bomber's vehicle, turning it into thousands of pieces of shrapnel. All that was left of the car was the front

Elder Jackson stands between two LDS soldiers, Brothers Satterthwaite and Thaden.

chassis, and it was one hundred meters down the street from the crater.

The security portion of our convoy functioned admirably. They quickly cordoned off the site and secured it while getting all of us into another armored vehicle and off to the airport as quickly as possible. Within a few minutes we had left the scene and were soon at the airport and the military base there. It was good to feel safe! I then had the chance to check everyone over and found, to our great relief, that there were no serious injuries. I didn't have a mark on me. All of us were fine. I am still in awe that we all walked away from that scene.

I was saddened by the unfortunate loss of innocent life and the grief that those families must have felt. I was confused and appalled at individuals who can perpetrate such crimes on others in the name of religion. Hate is strong.

This experience demonstrated to me what our friends in uniform are threatened with every single day. I had a small glimpse into their lives. I appreciate them all the more for their sacrifices and bravery.

I am thankful for brave and well-trained individuals who helped keep us safe and cared for. I am thankful for "level 7" armored vehicles (like a tank)! I am most thankful for the gospel and the comfort it supplies in incredibly challenging and difficult times. It has been like having a personal escort with me. I am thankful for things of lasting worth in a world where everything is throwaway, a world where nothing is guaranteed and none of us knows what will happen five minutes from now. What comfort! I cannot adequately express my gratitude for the gospel of Christ and its sure foundation when all around me is shaking and unsure.

EDITOR'S POSTSCRIPT

Following the incident, a military detail was sent to review the scene and examine the wreckage. One of those participating in the inspection was a member of the Church. This member later reported that he did not know how anyone could have survived that blast. Among the wreckage, this brother found only two remaining items belonging to Elder Jackson: a picture of his wife and his scriptures, which were burned around the edges. Commenting on these scriptures, Elder Jackson said, "I now have a new set of scriptures, but I will never discard my old ones."

Some time after this traumatic experience, Elder Jackson recorded the following contemplative thoughts in his journal:

> Days of serious soul-searching and introspection have followed. The sunrise of each new day is sweet, the love of my wife, family, fellow Saints and the Savior are strong. I'm thankful for a Heavenly Father who is real and interested. I have much yet to do and am grateful for each new minute. "And if our lives are spared again, to see the Saints their rest obtain, / Oh, how we'll make this chorus swell: All is well, All is well." My heart bleeds for the innocent and thanks God for the plan of salvation and its hero/champion, Jesus Christ.

---

* *In addition to his work with the U.S. Foreign Service, Elder Jackson served as an Area Seventy, with assignment over Afghanistan.*

TRANSPORTING AN AREA SEVENTY

Gerald C. Brady
Civilian Contractor
Afghanistan 2005–2008

Gerald Brady serving in Afghanistan

I was assigned the responsibility of arranging the transportation of Elder William K. Jackson across nearly fifty miles of dangerous terrain. Organizing an area conference in a war zone was a lengthy and stressful experience. This experience testified of my need to exercise faith and allow myself to be led by the Spirit to accomplish the otherwise impossible.

Elder Jackson, the Area Seventy stationed in New Delhi, India, and assigned over Afghanistan, contacted me and indicated that he wanted to have a conference with all of the LDS servicemen in Afghanistan on Sunday, November 13, 2005. The meeting would be held at Bagram Air Base, about fifty miles northeast of Kabul. He asked if the members of the Kabul LDS group could provide transportation for him to Bagram. Although this would be a simple task in the States, I knew this would not be easily accomplished in a war zone. As we proceeded to make arrangements, difficulties continued to mount.

In order to travel out in the "countryside," a military convoy must be organized and authorized. A convoy requires at least two vehicles, and each vehicle must carry two shooters. Each vehicle is assigned a code name (we chose "Moroni One" and "Moroni Two"). The series of events that allowed me to reserve the transport vehicles we needed could have been accomplished only by divine intervention. Finding the required four shooters was also a difficult task. Although I finally identified four individuals, at the last minute one gave notice that she would not be available. While I was considering what to do, to my relief another shooter approached and offered to help if she could have a ride. Another blessing.

The day after Elder Jackson arrived, we met for our normal weekly church meeting. Following the sacrament, Elder Jackson gave us a report on the video conference meeting he had attended just thirty-six hours earlier with the Quorum of the Twelve, the Church military relations committee, and various priesthood leaders throughout the world. The subject of the meeting was how the Church was serving military members in Iraq, Afghanistan, and other, smaller regions of the world. Elder Jackson reported that the Brethren were truly concerned for the welfare of those who are serving in war zones. Elder Jackson gave strong witness to the love expressed by Church leaders for the servicemen and women. My heart was touched that we could share in hearing his report.

The morning of the scheduled Afghanistan conference, we again had a problem securing the fourth shooter necessary for our convoy. After inquiring unsuccessfully around camp, I was prompted to ask for assistance from

Chief Leslie, an acquaintance of mine. I recalled that his name had come to my mind several times earlier as someone who might be able to help. As I began to search for him I heard a voice from behind me, "Were you looking for me?" I turned around and it was Chief Leslie. After receiving approval from his commander, he accompanied us on our journey. We again received Heavenly Father's help in finding adequate assistance to make the journey.

With everyone and everything organized, we were finally ready to leave our compound and escort Elder Jackson to the conference. Just at that moment, we were told that our base had been placed in lockdown because of a demonstration underway outside of the walls. No one was permitted to leave the base. Then a voice told me that we could get out the south gate. I ran to the south gate and received special permission from the gate commander for us to leave. I ran back to notify our group and we swiftly proceeded to the south gate. When we arrived, all vehicles were stopped. The gate commander apologized to me and said, "Sir, just after you left they called and shut down the gate. I'm sorry; I can't let you out! Have you tried the north gate? It might be open." I knew from experience that the north gate was almost never open. That gate is not even manned. Still, we quickly headed to the north gate and were relieved to find that it was open. A convoy of Humvees was returning from an off-compound mission, and they were allowed to reenter our camp via the north gate. Without asking if we could leave, we immediately exited the base and had an uneventful, albeit stressful, drive to Bagram. The Spirit had provided me with information needed to leave the compound and make the journey to the conference.

We arrived about ten minutes late for the conference in Bagram. Thirty members were waiting in the chapel for the meeting to begin. They were all a little concerned about our late arrival. I was asked to sit up front with their group leadership and Elder Jackson. Everything was going fine until the one conducting the meeting leaned over and asked me to speak for about five minutes. My mind scrambled on what I might say. I decided to focus on Nephi's words, where he said that he "went forth" being "led by the Spirit, not knowing beforehand the things which I should do" (1 Nephi 4:6, 7). That scripture seemed to define our journey to the conference. I then encouraged all present to use their time in Afghanistan to their advantage and not put their membership in the Church on hold while being deployed. I testified that each of us can be led by the Spirit to those things that will allow us to improve our standing before God. We should find a weakness and then overcome it and thereby become masters of ourselves. Although we cannot attend a temple during deployment, we should remain or become temple worthy.

Elder Jackson gave a wonderful talk. He took his remarks from King Benjamin's discourse in Mosiah. I remained captive during his talk and enjoyed being taught by him. The spirit was strong and vibrant. It was a wonderful opportunity to serve and be with one of Heavenly Father's great leaders, clearly an opportunity of a lifetime.

THE CHILDREN CLUNG TO US

Eugene "Gene" J. Wikle
Civilian Mentor to Ministry of Defense
and Afghan National Police
Iraq and Afghanistan, 2006–

In May 2006, I had the opportunity to perform a community service project delivering food and toys to an Afghan refugee camp. We began with a convoy briefing and were assigned to one of three convoy teams. The first convoy team was comprised of armed military personnel who would deploy first to establish a security perimeter around the refugee camp prior to our arrival.

The refugee camp is located west of Kabul. We departed at 0830 and arrived at the camp at 0900. We had to wear body armor while traveling to and from the camp. When we arrived at the camp, we were allowed to remove our body armor. I was assigned to the second convoy team. Our mission was to deliver toys to the children and play with them while the donated food was delivered to the adult refugees by the third convoy team.

Many of the refugees live in a bombed-out multistory building, although some live in tents. They have no electricity. Their water is located outside the building.

We estimated that there were between seventy-five to one hundred children in the camp. We delivered coloring books, crayons, soccer balls, soft

Gene Wikle and a refugee boy who appreciated the toys and loving affection

footballs, soft rubber balls, dolls, balloons, kites, and bubble soap toys. When we arrived and the children saw that we had toys, we were mobbed. To say they were excited would be an understatement. But even though they appreciated the toys, what they wanted most was to play with us and to be held by us. The children just clung to us, held our hands, wanted to be picked up and held. Many of them gave me a kiss on the cheek. It was a very humbling experience.

We spent an hour distributing the toys, playing with the children, and delivering the food. When it was time to leave, the children lined up along the road to wave good-bye. Most of the children gave our team members a kiss on the cheek and a bouquet of flowered grass they had picked from the field. No translation was necessary when I held these sweet children in my arms. Their smiles and hugs said it all.

This experience was another testimony of the cruelty of war and of how Satan has brought about so much destruction and disparity into the lives of our Father in Heaven's children. Life for these refugees is a day-to-day struggle for survival. I hope the continued donations of food and clothing will eventually lead these good people to a better life.

I have come to appreciate that the good people of Iraq and Afghanistan are children of our Father in Heaven. I have grown to love these people. I continue to hope and pray for their safety and success in becoming a self-sustaining nation, a nation that will allow the gospel of Jesus Christ to roll forth from border to border. As I have lived with these good people for over two years, I have come to appreciate and understand how much they need the gospel. Every day it is a blessing to serve the Lord and his children. This is truly one of the most satisfying experiences in my life. I am a servant of the Lord, and I am humbly going about my Father in Heaven's business in his vineyard of Afghanistan.

AN AMERICAN VETERAN MEETS AN IRAQI VETERAN: NEW FRIENDS AND BROTHERS

Eugene "Gene" J. Wikle
**Civilian Mentor to Ministry of Defense
and Afghan National Police**

Iraq and Afghanistan, 2006–

I was serving as a senior mentor and instructor to the Iraq Ministry of Defense. My assignment was to train the new Iraq acquisition and logistics senior leadership at the Ministry of Defense. Our training was conducted at the Baghdad Convention Center inside the infamous Green Zone. During the convention, a booth was set up outside my classroom. This booth was for a disabled Iraq veterans' organization. During one of my class breaks I left my classroom and saw a group of disabled men sitting at the table. I was immediately drawn to them. Not able to speak Arabic, I returned to my classroom to ask my interpreter to translate for me. I presented each of the disabled veterans with a military patch. I wanted to share the brotherhood of one veteran with another veteran. I was warmly greeted by these men who had lost limbs during the Iraq–Iranian War and the Persian Gulf War.

At the table sat Muneer Al Hosayny. Muneer had served in the Iraq Army during the early stages of the 1980–1988 Iraq–Iranian war. In that conflict Muneer was severely injured, resulting in the loss of both of his legs.

While serving in Iraq, Gene Wikle had the opportunity to spend an hour with Geraldo Rivera on a live Fox News broadcast from Iraq.

Before his injuries, Muneer was engaged to be married to an Iraqi woman. But when he became injured, family and friends strongly discouraged Muneer and his fiancée from getting married. They thought that Muneer would not be able to support himself or a family. Muneer and his fiancée loved each other very much. They are an example of "love conquers all." Through their love and determination they did marry. The results are shown below. (I refer to this family as my "happy Iraqi LDS family"—a hope and prayer for the future.)

Muneer and his wife are now the proud parents of three sons and three daughters. I later learned that he had been appointed by the Iraqi government to serve as the director of the Iraqi Disabled Veterans Organization. Muneer also explained to me that the U.S. Army had renovated a building for him to use for the Iraqi Disabled Veterans Organization.

Muneer and I exchanged photos of our families. I have a beautiful photo of Muneer's family. Muneer is an accomplished athlete. He coaches and plays on a wheelchair basketball team in Baghdad. He also participates in a disability Olympics competition. He is a javelin and shot-put competitor. He has shared with me photos of his Olympic competition and basketball team.

Muneer demonstrated to me that he is a man of God and through his faith, determination, courage, and love of family, he is an example for all of us.

Through our friendship we discussed our faith in God. We became good friends, friends for life. To this day, I still exchange email messages with Muneer. My first message from Muneer was sent to me while I was home in Arizona on leave. Below is his message. His English is not perfect in this message, but his friendship shines through.

August 16, 2004—Message from Muneer Al Hosayny—My Iraqi Brother

In the name of God—Dear Mr. Gene Wikle,

You don't know how much we suffer from the pain of your missing and your love. If we know about that we didn't permit you to go. We make the date of you are the sadden day. I know it daily and make a party with my pains. I don't believe I miss you because you are beside me always and you are spirit guard me and you are pictures is not image but it is fact. I'm live with it with you. I hope from my God to safely arrive and stay and come back. Thank you for everything.

After returning to Iraq, I had a special experience involving my friend Muneer. I recorded the experience in my journal, dated October 6, 2004:

Today at 12:30, I felt the need to go to the Baghdad Conference Center. I did not know why but I felt the urge to go. I did not have any appointments with anyone. I followed the promptings and proceeded to travel on the shuttle bus from the Embassy to the Conference Center.

As the bus was approaching the Convention Center my cell phone rang. An Iraqi woman at the Conference Center was on the phone translating for Muneer. He was at the Conference Center and needed to see me urgently. I told the translator that I would be there in five minutes. When I entered the Conference Center, Muneer was waiting for me on the first floor. With him were two men that I had not met before. One older gentleman was dressed as a sheik. Very distinguished looking (Omar Sharif?). When he greeted me I immediately noticed that both of his arms were missing. He had two artificial arms/hands made of fiberglass. He greeted me warmly. The other Iraqi man had an artificial leg. He also warmly greeted me.

Muneer explained through a translator that the Iraqi National Guard had to take possession of their veterans disability center. This center had been refurbished by the U.S. military. Muneer wanted me to ask the Embassy and U.S. military to help him and his friends find another facility. I told him that I would contact the Embassy to see if there is anything that can be done to help him. I told him that I could not guarantee that I would be successful but that I would at least inquire for him. He was happy with my commitment to at least inquire. I told Muneer that I was prompted by the Spirit to come to the Convention Center. Muneer said that he had prayed that I would come to him today. His prayers were answered.

I am grateful to have listened to the promptings of the Spirit. These are the experiences that leave a testimony in my heart that the people of Iraq need our help and want us to help them. I have grown to love the Iraqi people. I hope and pray that our efforts will help to bring peace and the gospel of Jesus Christ to these good people.

MY SICKNESS WAS A BLESSING

Senior Master Sergeant John C. "Clay" Gardner
U.S. Air Force
Afghanistan, August 2006–October 2007

I had a four-day pass and was scheduled to travel with a convoy to Bagram. We left at 8:00 A.M. I was crammed into the back of a small, unarmored SUV with two army gentlemen; one was a very big guy. It was going to be a very snug ride.

We started down the Jalalabad Road and missed a turn. We continued going until we ran out of paved road. From then on we endured unlimited potholes at thirty to forty miles an hour. We were getting tossed around like clothes in a washing machine. I had to roll my window down a bit because I started getting carsick. Then I thought of how I had heard of folks getting sick as a warning before danger as a gift from the Spirit. I wondered if I was getting carsick or if I was getting a warning. About that time the lieutenant colonel who was sitting in the back seat with me shouted at the assistant convoy commander to get on the radio and have the lead vehicle with the convoy commander pull over. The lieutenant colonel announced that he was taking command of the convoy from the lieutenant, who obviously wasn't sure how to get to Bagram.

We turned around and headed back across the same pothole-infested dirt roads. The incredibly bumpy roads had me dry heaving to the point of

31

almost losing my breakfast. I asked Heavenly Father to help us stop, if at all possible, so I could recover. A few moments later, the new convoy commander, Lieutenant Colonel Howard Malone, who had moved to the lead vehicle and was driving it, called us on the radio to let us know we were going to stop at Camp Phoenix to top off our gas. I knew Heavenly Father was looking out for me, and I felt the Spirit as I thanked him.

After enduring some more hardships, we eventually made it to Bagram. There we were informed that the road we were on reportedly had a suicide bomber driving around looking for a convoy to attack. I'm thankful we got off that road and made it to our destination.

GUITARS AND GOOD MUSIC

Senior Master Sergeant John C. "Clay" Gardner
U. S. Air Force
Afghanistan, August 2006–October 2007

I took my guitar with me on my deployment because I wanted to pass my downtime enjoyably. Once I had arrived on base it didn't take long before I found a few guys who were interested in forming a band. Our preference was to perform classic rock songs and have a good time. Word got around that there was a decent rock band on base. Soon we were getting invitations to play for different organizations, including the U.S. embassy. A highlight performance for us was when we played for four hundred servicemen at the Kabul International Airport. Our stage was a tractor trailer, and barbeque was served for everyone. The evening was great for morale, especially mine.

One day during our practice, a soldier came up to us and explained that a guitar manufacturer had sent him a guitar. He didn't know how to play, so he asked if we could give him some lessons. The thought then occurred to me, "Maybe there are people back in the States who could help us with our band's equipment." Our equipment was low quality or defective, making it hard to produce a good sound at our shows. I shared our situation with several music manufacturers back home, and nearly half of them responded, offering their assistance. Not only did our band get the needed music equipment, but we also received enough additional instruments to outfit the base's

John Gardner plays lead guitar and sings with his band at one of his many concerts for the soldiers.

chapel and the Morale, Welfare, and Recreation Office.

I know music has a special emotional connection for people. For days after each of our performances, dozens of people will come up to me, shake my hand, and say, "Thank you for helping me forget about where I am for a few hours." It gives me a warm feeling to know I gave some folks a good time with music from our American culture. Rather than making them feel homesick, it helps them feel that they can get through another six weeks, six months, or however long they have left on deployment.

I have a testimony that music has power either to uplift or discourage. If there is ever a questionable word in the songs I play, I will find an acceptable substitution for that word. I will not sing what I consider to be foul language or a song with a degrading message. I have done that with every band I have played in. No one has ever complained or asked me to sing the original word. I think it is the right thing to do. I play rock songs that are meaningful, upbeat, and fun. I don't expect that what I did in my band would have converted anyone, but I do know it provided comfort and a little bit of fun to people who really needed a positive distraction.

BUILDING A UNIVERSITY

J. Garth Thompson

Ph.D., Mechanical and Nuclear Engineering
Kansas State University and Kabul University, 2007–

The university in Afghanistan's capital city, Kabul, does not have a very high education level. Among the many problems plaguing the university are faculty and facility issues. I was among several professors who traveled to Kabul University to assess the situation and to determine what kind of help it needed. Of the many professors considered for the job, I was the one the university administrators selected to help them build their engineering department. Many people from around the world have helped by sending equipment and supplies. Yet all the supplies were useless because no one came here to stay and help them put all the pieces together. Our commitment to the university is to stay and help the people work through the problems until they are able to function as a vibrant engineering department.

I do a little bit of everything, but my focus is on mentoring, building laboratories, forming curriculum, and simply making things happen. The Lord is helping me make things happen. A lot of things seem to happen spontaneously, as the right people arrive at just the right time. For example, one day we were discussing the kind of furniture we needed for portions of the building, including the classrooms. The high-quality furniture we selected was from Japan. Two days after we selected the furniture, a representative

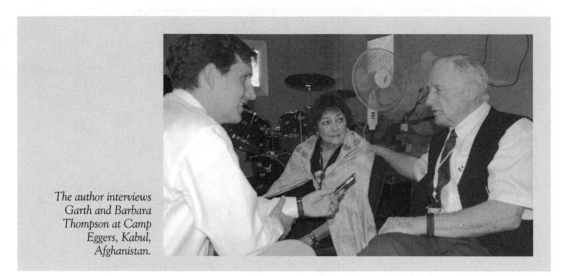

The author interviews Garth and Barbara Thompson at Camp Eggers, Kabul, Afghanistan.

from the same Japanese furniture manufacturer showed up unannounced. We never contacted him; he just showed up and informed us that his company wanted to donate furniture to the university!

On another occasion, we were struggling to get our internet fiber-optic connections installed. As we were considering how to accomplish this highly technical task, a qualified professional offered his assistance and quickly completed the job. Such blessings have happened repeatedly. Just as we discover a need, someone appears out of the blue to make it happen.

We treat our time here as we would a mission for the Church. We feel the Lord wants us here, and with His help we will succeed.

EDITOR'S POSTSCRIPT

Of her husband, Sister Barbara Thompson has said, "I am with him when he says his prayers. He prays about the success of his assignment at the university. He is very sincere in the words he chooses. He does not use memorized phrases but speaks from his heart. My husband talks to Heavenly Father about the specific items he needs to make things progress here. He asks for specific things, and I believe his prayers are the source of the great success he is having here. We have seen so many things happen that are truly incredible."

BLESSINGS IN A BACKPACK

Major Michael Burton Howard

U.S. Air Force

Iraq, April–September 2007

A girl attending the school for refugees discovers the contents of her gift bag.

I served in Kirkuk, Iraq, which culturally is a very diverse city. Every ethnic group in Iraq can be found in Kirkuk—Kurd, Shia Arab, Sunni Arab, Turkoman, and Assyrian Christian. When people see our convoys, they go out of their way to smile and wave. Although the ethnic divisions often create tensions, most people just want to live in peace. They are grateful to us for saving them from Saddam Hussein's tyrannical regime. That is why I have so much hope for that country.

The air force chaplain's office at Kirkuk Regional Air Base has a project called Operation Outreach. It is a program through which school

Major Michael Howard among a classroom of school children opening bags of school supplies

supplies are sent to Iraqi school children in need. People from all over the United States gather the standard items that would go into a school child's backpack—pencils, pens, paper, crayons, and sometimes a Beanie Baby— and send them to the chaplain's office in Kirkuk.

My unit was one of the few air force units authorized to go off base and into the city. Early in my deployment we organized convoys to two schools in Kirkuk. The first school was an all-girls school (kindergarten through high school) that had been the site of a recent car bomb. Insurgents had targeted a police station without any regard to the school located directly across the street. In the attack, many students were wounded and a few killed. Because of this, we decided to visit the school and provide some comfort. We loaded up hundreds of packets to ensure we had enough for each child. My men were greeted warmly by many school and city officials. During their visit, my men heard stories of tragedy and courage about teachers and girls who helped save the lives of the injured and grieved for their dead. They truly appreciated the assistance we brought, both in the form of school supplies and through our direct military force against the insurgents and terrorists.

The second school we visited was a school for refugees, both boys and girls, kindergarten through high school. They were all very poor, and we felt we could accomplish much good there. As always, my men were wearing tactical armored vests and drop holsters on their legs, and they were carrying machine guns. With this appearance, we entered the school smiling and carrying over four hundred loaded bags for the children. It was an imposing sight to see big men wearing body armor and carrying radios and loaded M-4 rifles, all smiling while giving away school supplies. Amazingly, the kids were in no way intimidated. They were growing up in a time of war and they knew the good guys from the bad guys. Despite our appearance, they came running up to us yelling, "The Americans are here!"

After the initial greeting, it became a very intimate event. We went from classroom to classroom. We were allowed to introduce ourselves and our purpose. We would say in each classroom, "People in America care about the future of Iraq, and that means they care about you. So the people in America want to help by giving you school supplies." We then went to *each child* while they all sat at their desks and presented each one with a bag of school supplies. Their eyes lit up every time. They were so grateful.

When I go home to the States and see children going to school with their backpacks, I am going to think about how blessed they are to have even the most simple things, such as paper, crayons, and a backpack to carry them in. Operation Outreach wasn't without danger—it's always a risk to go off-base in Iraq—but it was worth it to give hope and comfort to these hundreds of beautiful Iraqi children.

BLANKETS WARM VICTIMS

Major Michael Burton Howard

U.S. Air Force

Iraq, April–September 2007

With less than one month left in my deployment, my aunt and her daughter-in-law organized a girls' camp project to make twelve blankets for people in need. These large, soft fleece blankets were handmade with loving care and sent to me for distribution. As I thought about who should receive the blankets, I remembered a recent car bombing in downtown Kirkuk. I thought it would be meaningful if we could find victims of the attack and let them know that Americans care and were thinking of them. A friend of mine who served as the provincial police chief went to work and identified several families directly affected by the attack.

The location of the families posed a real and dangerous threat. Kirkuk can be an unpredictable, menacing city. This mission was unique because my team was going to rely on the police chief to guide and escort our convoy without us knowing beforehand exactly where our route would take us. We had to trust him. Most of my men were uneasy about not being in complete control and not inclined to trust any Iraqi official completely. As we gathered and prepared to leave the base, I had to make a judgment call. I was in command, and it was up to me to decide whether to proceed or not. I relied on inspiration from the Holy Ghost, and I believed we were going to be fine. I

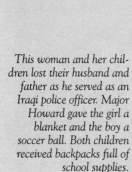

This woman and her children lost their husband and father as he served as an Iraqi police officer. Major Howard gave the girl a blanket and the boy a soccer ball. Both children received backpacks full of school supplies.

felt we were going to return safely and that we needed to accomplish this mission. I went from Humvee to Humvee and said, "Guys, I know you are uncomfortable, but we are going to be fine on this mission. Trust me on this one. We are going to be safe." The Holy Ghost's comfort enabled me to gain the confidence of these tremendous men.

The mission took us through the narrow city streets, around piles of rubble, and under drooping telephone wires strung like spaghetti between the old buildings. We knocked on the dwelling doors and were introduced through our Iraqi linguists as "Americans who would like to provide your family with comfort." We proceeded to give those blankets of love to families who had lost a loved one in the attacks. If there were children in the home, we also gave them backpacks filled with school supplies, soccer balls, and stuffed animals. I would take as many as I could by the hand, look at them, and say, "May God bless and protect you." It was my way to exercise my priesthood and bless them in a small way. Frequently, other children would swarm us, and so we were prepared to share the supplies, Beanie Babies, and soccer balls with them, too.

I have always trusted the Lord and learned to rely on the Holy Ghost,

Major Howard and Buri-yar, a nine-year-old boy who was grateful for a gift of a soccer ball. His family expressed gratitude to all Coalition Forces for freeing them from Saddam.

especially as a young missionary in Italy. Now, like then, the reassurance of the Spirit came to me. I was able to safely lead my men while serving the people of Kirkuk.

To end my deployment on such a high note, with a humanitarian mission, was very special. We were doing what we could to give hope and comfort to these children of our Heavenly Father who were so tragically deprived of their husbands, brothers, and fathers in this war. I will never forget their tears and their gratitude and encouragement to us. They pleaded with us to keep on fighting for their freedom and give them hope that their country would someday be like America.

AN INSPIRED EULOGY

Major Michael Burton Howard
U.S. Air Force
Iraq, April–September 2007

Captain Degn, our LDS chaplain, shared a very poignant message one Sunday in sacrament meeting. The army had lost some soldiers in battle earlier in the week. Among the fallen was an LDS soldier belonging to our small congregation. Chaplain Degn reminded us that being a member of The Church of Jesus Christ of Latter-day Saints was not a guarantee that we would not be wounded or killed in war. He counseled that *how* we lived our lives is what is important, that we should be faithful to the gospel and "soldier on" by doing our duty.

Those are sobering words. I think all present pondered their own mortality. Sometimes the Spirit is sent to prompt us to action to save our lives. At other times our lives are not spared. We return to the God who created us, and the Spirit is sent to comfort those who remain. The test of our faith is to submit ourselves to the Lord's will in all things, even giving our very lives if he requires it. Will we then keep our faith? Will we trust that the Lord has a plan for each of us and accept what he has designed for us?

In my own life at the time, I had been through a great trial of faith as I sought to reconcile my will with the Lord's will. I had had the most difficult week of my life. I was in command of Expeditionary Detachment 2410 of the

Major Howard (left) and a member of his team on patrol

Air Force Office of Special Investigations (AFOSI). My unit's mission was to identify insurgent cells and find ways to neutralize them. We were very good at this. As federal agents, the men under my command were experts in the use of counterintelligence methods and police tactics. But the best training in the world is no guarantee in war.

On Tuesday, June 5, 2007, I was notified that I needed to report immediately to the medical facility on base. Men under my command, while on their daily convoy mission in downtown Kirkuk, had been hit by a roadside bomb. As I arrived at the 506th Expeditionary Medical Squadron, I learned from my unit's superintendent that the first vehicle of our three-vehicle convoy had taken a direct hit by a powerful armor-penetrating bomb, which had ripped through the vehicle. I rushed inside and watched as the medical staff worked on three of my men in the emergency room. It was a horrible scene, and I did not know if any of them would live. I joined my other men in the break room. We did our best to comfort each other as we waited for any kind of news. The doctor finally entered the room and explained that, unfortunately, they had been able to save only one of the men. We lost two very fine men and good friends that day.

The ensuing days became a nonstop parade of demands on my time and energy. I had to answer endless inquiries relating to the attack, attend to hundreds of details related to the final affairs of my fallen men, arrange care and support services for my surviving men, and find solutions to get my unit back on its feet and fully mission capable again. I had to remain strong for the sake of my surviving men and the success of my unit. The base commander depended on us to successfully neutralize insurgents in our assigned area, for the protection of the base. We had to get back out there. Giving up would be cowardly and unacceptable. I felt the tremendous weight of responsibility and a measure of irrational "survivor's guilt," which is common to many military commanders who find themselves in these circumstances.

I began working with a Catholic chaplain to organize the memorial service scheduled to take place the following Friday. As the commander, it was my duty to deliver a eulogy in tribute to the two men who were killed while under my command. I had three days to write it, but at the end of each day I was exhausted and had no sense of what I should say. The night before the memorial service, I still had no idea where to begin. As I finished my other duties at a little past midnight, I knelt and prayed, "Heavenly Father, I do not know what to say and I have run out of time. I need help."

The help came. During my prayer, I remembered reading a passage attributed to Tecumseh, the great Shawnee chief and statesman, titled, "To Live As a Warrior." It was in a book that had been given to me at the beginning of my deployment to Iraq. I pulled the book off the shelf and flipped right to the passage. I read the words again and knew they were perfect for the occasion. They described these two men perfectly, and I knew I had found the spiritual center of my eulogy. As I began to write, words came to my mind, and I suddenly knew what to say about each of my fallen special agents. Once again, as always in my life, when I needed the Lord, he was there. I *know* I did not write that eulogy alone but received a portion of his Spirit, which lent inspiration, hope, and comfort in my time of need.

The Catholic chaplain was the first to review my eulogy, which had to be officially approved before I would be allowed to deliver it at the memorial service. He shared with me how he had been praying that I would find the right things to say. After reading my words, he felt his prayer had been answered.

As the memorial service began, I was literally beyond the limits of my strength. The week's demands had drained me, both physically and emotionally. At military memorial services in Iraq, there is a traditional way a soldier's or airman's photo, helmet, and rifle are arranged on a sandbag stand. As commander, it was my duty to place a folded flag in front of each of these symbolic displays. My knees were literally shaking as I placed the first flag. I felt that I was going to fall from exhaustion. I silently prayed, "Lord, I need strength. I do not want to fall and dishonor these men."

My prayer was answered. I received strength in my legs, and I was able to render the proper military honors and then take my place at the podium to speak. I received strength in my voice as I delivered my eulogy. As I looked on the audience, I saw all of the members of my own unit, and many others present, nodding with each sentence I spoke. They had tears in their eyes, and though they were tears of sadness, they also were tears of comfort and hope in an eternal life. The Comforter attended us. I knew my eulogy was not perfect, but I hoped it was worthy of these courageous men.

After the service, many shook my hand and thanked me for saying words they needed to hear. I was reassured that with the Lord's help, I had risen to the occasion for the sake of these fine men and their families, who would receive a recording of the service.

As an air force officer, I will always feel some responsibility for the deaths and injuries of the members of my command. As a warrior, I felt great satisfaction in carrying out my duties by quickly returning my unit to full mission capability and redressing those injuries to the insurgents who had carried out that terrible attack on my unit's convoy. I echo Captain Moroni in asserting that we would not shed their blood if they did not come against us. As a priesthood holder, I am grateful for the lessons I learned as a young missionary, to place my trust in the Lord and enjoy the gift of the Holy Ghost.

ANOTHER ZION'S CAMP?

First Lieutenant David DeMille
U.S. Army
Afghanistan, March 2006–March 2007

One time our convoy was out on night patrol. We stopped by what was known as a "district center." The district center compound was the location of the area's main Afghan government buildings and police station. It was normal for us to occasionally visit this center at night. Normally we would arrive to find everyone asleep except a few guards. This night everyone was awake and in their defensive fighting positions. We asked what was going on

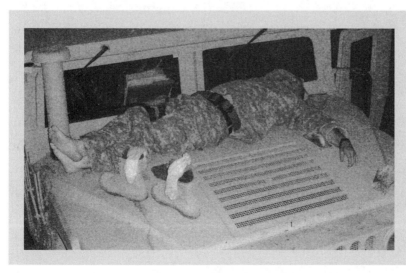

"At night while on patrol we were so tired we would lie down anywhere and fall asleep: on dirt, rocks, or the hood of our Humvee."—David DeMille

David DeMille holds a "night letter," which the Taliban distributes in front of people's doors at night. These letters typically threaten teachers, police, parents who send their daughters to school, or anyone assisting U.S. forces.

and they explained they had received intelligence indicating that they were going to be attacked that night. My convoy decided to stay and help them defend their post. We quickly did our best to hide our trucks in the compound so the enemy would not detect our presence. Since we did not have cots or beds, we slept on the ground or on the hoods of our trucks.

About halfway through the night it started to rain. The rain was literally pouring down. Within a few seconds, my guys were soaked head to toe. We scrambled into our trucks, but we were already drenched and miserable. We spent the rest of the night trying to sleep in wet and uncomfortable positions. The night slowly turned into morning without an attack. The next day we continued on our patrol route soaking, smelly, and miserable.

A few days later, I had the opportunity to visit a larger U.S. base and actually attend a Church meeting. I cannot remember all the details of the lesson, but it was about Church history and Zion's Camp. The instructor shared how a mob was coming to attack the Saints and that the Lord prevented the attack by sending a fierce storm. I then thought of the wet night I had just experienced. I do not know if we would have been attacked that night, but that same Afghan district center had been hit before—and it was hit again a few days after we were there. Even though the rain made us miserable, it may have prevented a violent attack. No one would have attacked in that horrible weather.

I have since thought that when something happens in our lives that makes us totally miserable, maybe God is intervening to keep us safe. Or maybe he is blessing us in a way we cannot immediately understand. Although we might be miserable for a time, in the long run, God might be doing his part to bless or save our lives.

"GOD BE WITH YOU TILL WE MEET AGAIN"

Chief Warrant Officer 2 Dennis Lorenz
U.S. Army Chinook Helicopter Pilot
Iraq, July 2007–

My first Sunday in Iraq was on the Balad Airfield base. It was fast Sunday, and during the sacrament meeting a brother shared a recent experience and his testimony. His words left a lasting impression on me. He explained that he was a civilian truck driver and had been serving in Iraq for nearly four years. For the last year, he was promised he could work exclusively in the safer, secured area known as "inside the wire." One day, his co-workers were shorthanded and needed a driver to accompany them on a long and potentially dangerous convoy mission. He was nervous about going because of recent IED attacks on convoys. He originally declined but later agreed to assist the team.

The day came, and he suited up in armor and climbed into his semitruck. With the engines running, all the vehicles were ready to leave the base. All drivers were listening to their two-way radios for final instructions. The air force radio operator on base broadcast final route details to the drivers and then concluded by saying, "God be with you till we meet again."

He wondered, "Why did the radio operator say those words? Were those

Chief Warrant Officer 2 Dennis Lorenz in front of a Chinook helicopter

words meant for me?" Those final words provided comfort to him during his dangerous mission.

After the convoy reached its destination, it immediately turned around and headed back to base. On their way back, another military convoy passed them heading in the opposite direction. Within five minutes, the second convoy was hit by an IED, killing seven. The blast occurred at a location where he'd been only moments before. As this brother arrived back on base, he immediately went to find the radio operator. He asked the operator why he had said, "God be with you till we meet again." The radio operator responded, "Because those words are a part of my faith." The driver hugged the man and said, "It is a part of my faith too. Thank you!"

The Spirit was there as this story was related. It was an emotional moment for all present. The timing of this story was very important for me because I was new to Iraq. This brother's story helped me to accept for the first time the real danger of my situation. His testimony inspired me from the very beginning of my deployment to have a hymn in my heart and its words in my mind. I fly helicopters outside the wire four or five times a week, and

I never leave without singing a hymn to myself. The hymns have definitely comforted me and soothed my nerves.

On three occasions, I have had close calls with catastrophe. One of these scary moments came when we had problems with in-flight aerodynamics. During such sudden and intense moments, flight crews refer to what happens to their bodies as a "pucker factor." This is when all the muscles in your body are in a tense, defensive state. As I was piloting through one such moment, everyone on board was in that pucker factor—except me. I did not have that feeling. Instead, I had a feeling of being hugged—and I did not worry. We were able to get out of that situation and everyone collected themselves. When I brought the helicopter in to land, I had the same feeling of comfort and knew there was no problem. I am grateful that the Spirit was with me.

LOOKING INTO THE EYES OF PRISONERS

Major Bruce G. Flint

Washington Army National Guard

Iraq, 2004

As an optometrist, I had the opportunity to travel around Iraq providing eye care to soldiers, Iraqi civilians, and detainees in prison. I was the only optometrist on our base, so I stayed very busy. One day a medical commander asked me if I would be willing to visit different prisons and examine detainees. He explained that the Red Cross had asked us to provide eye care in the prisons. I said I would go if my commander so directed. He responded, "I know, but are you *willing* to go?" I agreed to be of assistance to anyone who needed me.

Once I agreed, I was told that my patients were going to be HVDs (High Value Detainees)—prisoners of special importance. Some of the eyes I examined belong to those featured on the "most-wanted Iraqi playing cards." These cards were issued by the U.S. military to help troops identify the most-wanted members of President Saddam Hussein's government.

To meet with these people and provide them with medical care was a very interesting experience. I had to ponder what I was about to do in my own mind prior to seeing them. At one time I thought, "Should I help these people?" I finally came to the conclusion that regardless of who they are and what atrocities they have done, they are still human beings. They are still children of our Father in Heaven. Without rationalizing their actions, I do

Standing in a tent that served as a chapel are (left to right): Assistant Group Leader Lieutenant Colonel Evans, Group Leader Colonel Moore, and Assistant Group Leader Major Flint.

not believe they should be treated like animals. The actions of others don't determine how you must react to them. With that in mind, it was not hard for me to perform my duty.

When I first arrived, not many patients had signed up to see me. My first few patients went back and told the other prisoner-patients that I was a nice doctor who cared. The next day I had more patients, and my numbers tripled the third day. I put in some long hours. One of my final patients was Saddam Hussein. When I was examining him I did not want him to think he was getting any notoriety, and so I treated him with the same courtesy I did all my patients. He was respectful to me but seemed very old and depressed. Considering the background of those whom I examined, I was pleasantly surprised at the courtesy and politeness shown to me.

I will never forget what they all did after the examination. Before leaving the room, each prisoner placed his right hand over his heart and bowed. Each one, without fail, made this sincere expression of gratitude. They did not have to do this, but they did. That really had an impact on me. One prisoner expressed his gratitude in a very unique way. The prisoners were not allowed to have anything to write with. So he created watercolors from the food coloring on Skittles candy pieces. He collected the Skittles from MREs (Meal, Ready-to-Eat), placed them in a drop of water, and used the dye as

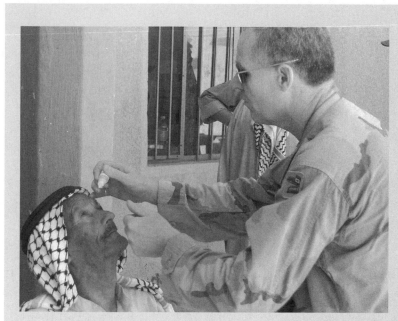

Major Flint administers eye drops to an Iraqi patient.

watercolor paint. Using "Skittles paint" and a stick, he painted a picture for me as a way to say "thank you."

I was there to provide medical attention, not to judge them. However, in the back of my mind I thought about how the Lamanites were at times a "blood-thirsty people" (Mosiah 10:12). Their traditions, culture, and teachings led many astray, and yet when they were taught the gospel many embraced it wholly. Maybe under different circumstances some of these people may have turned out differently.

During my hundreds of examinations I never felt threatened except for one time. I felt very uncomfortable around this one individual. He just seemed to have a different aura around him. I certainly felt that he was someone I had to be on guard with. It is said that the eye is the window to the soul. I do not necessarily believe that adage. I did not need to look into his eyes to know what kind of person he was. I do not think anyone needs to look into the eyes to be able to discern. The Spirit alone can direct you.

DON'T GO BACK WITH THEM

Henry Zander
Civilian Contractor
Iraq and Afghanistan, 2006–

My first assignment in Iraq was my first experience in a combat zone. It was a daily occurrence on the base where I was staying, Balad Air Base, to have rocket or mortar attacks. One day in May 2004, I had worked the previous day, through the night, and into the next day. It was approaching lunch time and I was ready for bed. A few of my friends wanted me to go to lunch with them. Despite how tired I was, they persuaded me to go with them. The base was huge, so we drove a mile in our HMMWV, or Humvee. After lunch, we left the building and were walking back to our vehicle.

Humvee damaged by rocket attack

Henry Zander stands near 9/11 memorial.

As we approached the vehicle, I had a very strong impression. Actually, it was more than an impression. I recognized it as the Spirit saying, "Don't go back with them." The message was clear. So I stopped and said, "Hey, I am not going to go back with you guys."

My friends replied, "But you're tired and you want to go to bed. We will get you back in just a few minutes."

I thanked them but told them that I would find another way back. I ended up locating my vehicle, which another contractor had been borrowing, and drove it back to a location near my sleeping quarters. My friends arrived at their building and parked the vehicle. Ten seconds after they parked their vehicle, a 127mm rocket flew over their heads and blew up the chaplain's Humvee, which was parked two spaces over. The rocket pierced the soft skin of the Humvee body just behind the front left wheel and exploded directly beneath the engine. The vehicle actually capped much of the shrapnel and prevented collateral damage. My friends ran into an adjacent building, and one collapsed with exhaustion from the event.

We had multiple attacks throughout the day, which kept me up the rest of the day. It was late that night before I finally got to bed. Then I finally had time to reflect on the day's events. Only then did I realize that if I had ridden back with them, I would have exited the Humvee from the rear and walked directly to my quarters, which were exactly in line with the explosion. Considering the time it would have taken me to get out of the vehicle and head back to my room, I would have been at the *direct* point of impact. I then recalled the prompting I had received earlier that day that told me not to go back with my co-workers.

I know Heavenly Father is very aware of all of us. I knew that prior to this experience, but this just reinforced that knowledge. He lives; he absolutely lives. Being spared from the rocket explosion only confirmed what I already knew to be true.

TOY ANIMALS, STUFFED HOT WATER BOTTLES, AND LOVE

Kristine Stoehner

U.S. Army Corps of Engineers

Afghanistan, April–October 2007

One of the reasons I volunteered for deployment is that I was hoping to find a way to make a difference for the women of Afghanistan. The women in this country have been *so* oppressed for *so* long. This country has experienced nothing but war for the last thirty-five years. As their men were killed, the women became "a nothing." They had no legal rights and no money, and they still had children to support. My goal was to meet some of these women and learn how I could make a difference in their lives.

I have been able to make a difference with the Women of Hope Project. This amazing organization is run by an American woman named Betsy Beamon. She has devoted her life to the women of Afghanistan. She employs two hundred women with sewing projects. Their handmade goods are sold to sustain life for these women and their children. She teaches hydroponic gardening, which provides much of their life-sustaining food. She teaches women to become independent and has started a school for refugee children.

As soon as I learned of the Women of Hope Project, I knew I wanted to be involved. My stake Relief Society back home worked with me in organizing a huge service project. My stake collected over a thousand pounds of

Kristine Stoehner serves at a "Women of Hope" bazaar.

sewing materials for the women and school supplies for the children. It was a great project that directly blessed the lives of many women and children in need.

As soon as I return back home, I am going to start contacting hot water bottle manufacturers. I will also be seeking donated stuffed animals. These two items are simple, everyday items to us, but they will save precious lives in Afghanistan. The hot water bottles will be placed inside the stuffed animals, and the animals will be sewn back together. The completed items will be shipped to Afghanistan and distributed to women with very small children. This is a vital gift because one out of four newborns dies here. That grim reality is largely due to exposure. Placing the hot water bottles in the stuffed animals accomplishes two objectives. It provides a safe way for the infant to stay warm, and it also shares joy in the form of a toy.

I have a special connection to the plight of these women because I am a woman and because of what I have been taught in Relief Society. I am a convert to the Church, and the Relief Society introduced me to what it really means to provide charitable service. I love the united feeling of sisterhood I experience when I attend Relief Society. These acts of service to the women of Afghanistan are things I can do for those who are unable to be introduced formally to Christianity. However, by providing this service, the fruits of Christianity are being shared with them.

BRAHMS' LULLABY

Major Steven Olsen

U.S. Air Force

Neonatologist, Landstuhl Regional Medical Center, 2004–

Here in this large, sprawling hospital I take care of healthy and sick babies. A few years ago, we instigated the playing of Brahms' Lullaby over the entire hospital's sound system every time a baby is born. The twenty-second music segment alerts everyone of a new birth. We average about four births a day. It is an endearing tradition for most of the hospital staff.

The department that seems to enjoy hearing the lullaby the most is the intensive care unit (ICU). These amazing people deal with soldiers who have been traumatically injured in the war. One nurse shared with me how she received comfort from the soothing music and what it represents. She and the doctors had been intently working on a severely injured patient. Despite all their efforts to keep the patient alive, he passed away. As the loss weighed on their shoulders, they heard Brahms' Lullaby play softly over the speakers. The team who had been working together paused and reflected. Pondering on the birth of a baby provided them with a sense of peace and the eternal perspective of life and death.

My perspective of the war is a little different because I work with babies. I never forget that most of these baby's fathers are deployed downrange. Occasionally, a father will have permission to temporarily leave his duties

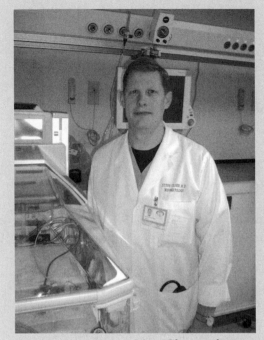

Major Olsen stands next to a newborn's warming bed.

and be at the hospital. I've seen instances where a father was in combat in Iraq and six hours later was beside his wife as she delivered their child. For the most part, however, the father is unable to return for the birth and may later miss the baby's first steps. Unfortunately, some fathers do not return from the war at all. When a father is absent because he is fulfilling his military duty, I witness a sacrifice made by both the father and the mother. This definitely makes me appreciate my life, my freedoms, and the sacrifice others are making for me.

I'M HERE TO SERVE

Sergeant Terry Chang
U.S. Army Reserve
Afghanistan, February 2006–March 2008

I decided to go back into the army for a silly reason by most sane people's standards—I wanted to experience war, and I wanted to go to Afghanistan to help people. The unit I was to go with is located in Pleasant Grove, Utah. It is a civil affairs unit. Its job is to help people, and that is what I wanted to do. We build roads, provide power/electricity through the construction of micro-hydro plants, and give assistance to the populace through the education of their society.

Sergeant Chang with Afghan civilians

I did not go to Afghanistan thinking everything would be fine and that my comrades and I would be welcomed with open arms. I've been fired upon and been in contact with the enemy on several occasions. However, Afghanistan is a beautiful country. The scenery is breathtaking and in many ways looks like Utah and Colorado. The people are friendly and peace loving for the most part; they are just trying to raise families and exist in peace. I have met and become friends with many of these people.

The downside of this country and its conflict is that many individuals here will try to kill me on sight. They want power only for themselves and will do anything to obtain that power, even if it means hurting or killing their fellow citizens. We build things for the people; others destroy the things we've built. They hurt people and their children; we take those victims to our

Sergeant Chang patrols the Afghan countryside.

hospitals to be helped. We, the soldiers, are also killed or injured in the process. Fatalities and injuries are a fact of war. Those things happen even to the best of people who choose to serve. I have had five friends who have been killed in combat over here. Their deaths have affected me greatly.

Death here is therefore a reality that I am very aware of. Every time I leave the wire, I carry both an M4 carbine and a 9mm automatic pistol. I also carry over three hundred rounds of ammunition. I lock and load my weapons every time I go out and then pray that I will never have to pull the trigger. To this date, I have never fired a round except in practice at a range. But I will if I have to, to protect myself or someone else who needs protection in an action.

Helaman's stripling warriors believed what their mothers taught them (see Alma 53). They believed, as I believe, that if one stays true to the faith and follows the admonitions of our Lord, that we can be kept safe from harm. I take the sacrament whenever I can; counsel other soldiers as needed; pray often every day for my safety, as well as that of the soldiers who serve with me; give priesthood blessings when asked; read the Book of Mormon every day; provide a good example to those around me; keep a daily journal; and bear testimony when the opportunity arises. I know the Book of Mormon is true. I know that Joseph Smith was a prophet of God. I know we continue to have a living prophet on the earth today and that he leads and guides this Church today. I know that Jesus is the Christ and that God lives.

EXAMINING THE ENEMY

Major Michael Duncan Jones

U.S. Army

Afghanistan, September 2004–February 2005

In addition to serving as brigade flight surgeon on Bagram Air Base, I also worked in the base hospital's emergency room and as the physician for the detainee facility. There were roughly six hundred prisoners in that holding facility. Some were hard-core terrorists, but most were just hired fighters, willing to kill for the highest paying warlord in their region. And some were probably innocent farmers, arrested only because they were not wise enough to avoid association with the first two groups. It was a large prison.

All of the prisoners were interrogated on a daily basis. My job was to examine each prisoner after the interrogations to ensure that no abuse was taking place. I spent three hours every morning examining these enemy combatants. During these examinations I observed many with smiles on their faces who had contrasting hatred and anger in their eyes. At times I sensed real evil when a prisoner was brought in to be examined, and the eyes were void of light. Mostly I just saw mistrust and sensed a profound weariness from these men who had known nothing but war, death, and disappointment for the past thirty years.

I was inspired on a daily basis as I participated in a team effort that provided world-class medical care to these enemy combatants. Many of them had had their lives saved by heroic first-aid given to them on the battlefield, where moments before they had been shooting to kill the same soldiers who now toiled to preserve their lives.

Some of my colleagues found it difficult to feel or show compassion to these men who had possibly killed our brothers in arms. Because of the gospel in my life, I did not have feelings of hate. I knew some of those I treated had made horrible decisions in their lives and had consequently lost the Light of Christ. I perceived that others, however, were not so entrenched in evil, and I hoped for their eternal salvation as sincerely as I hope for my own. I was motivated to be especially compassionate in my interactions with these enemy combatants, hoping that someday their hearts might be softened when they reflect on the quality of care provided them by Americans. Through my interpreter, I asked them about their wives and families. I took the time to make sure they understood how to take the medicine we gave them. I gave them counsel on how to take better care of themselves.

My goal was to defuse the hatred against America that was festering among these people by providing more than just courteous medical care. I hoped to make a human connection, to help them see me as I saw them, as sons of loving mothers, husbands of loving wives, and fathers of loving children.

If a solid case could not be made against certain prisoners, they were released. As many as forty prisoners a week were allowed to enter back into society. When these releases occurred each week, I hoped a few of my patients would leave, and that they would do so feeling motivated to give peace a chance in their nation, remembering a doctor who wanted to heal hearts as much as to bandage wounds.

I RAN FOR THEM!

Sergeant Jill Stevens *
Utah Army National Guard
Afghanistan, 2004

Sergeant Jill Stevens with an Afghan woman. In many cases, Afghan women will not allow their photo to be taken unless they are completely covered with their burqa.

My Utah National Guard unit was deployed with an infantry division from Hawaii. A few of the soldiers from Hawaii run in the world-famous Honolulu Marathon every year. Even though they were in Afghanistan, they thought it would be great for morale to create the inaugural Afghanistan Marathon sponsored by the Honolulu Marathon. The details were worked out and equipment, time clocks, and even banners were sent. The banner over the start/finish line stated boldly, "Honolulu Marathon."

We arrived at the marathon course in Chinook helicopters two hours before the race began. We were reminded that although security was

Sergeant Stevens completes one of her five laps at the marathon's start/finish line.

provided, the area was still a combat zone. A quick-reaction force was on hand to respond should an attack occur. A team of armored Humvees was ready to roll out of the gate on a moment's notice. Some of the guard towers doubled as water and aid stations. There were even holes dug along the course so runners had somewhere to flee if rockets or mortars were fired in their direction. Military participants had the option to run with their weapons. During the security briefing, I looked around at all the runners still wearing full body armor and thought, "What am I doing running a marathon *during a war?*"

With as many as 187 troops and civilians from around the country participating, we ran about five laps for a full 26.2 mile marathon. The course was a dirt-and-rock trail. The first three laps, I had energy and felt great. On the fourth lap my legs started to burn, and during the fifth lap I had nothing left. It was too hard.

Then it occurred to me what I was really doing. I thought that I was probably among the first group of women ever to run a marathon in Afghanistan. I was a woman running in a country where women are defiled and have no rights. As I ran, I began to focus on how Afghan women are treated. Feelings of anger and frustration came over me. The feelings that followed were centered on pride—pride not only to be in the military, but also to be a *woman* in the military fighting for the women of Afghanistan.

From then on, every step I took I was thinking and running for them. *This race is for them!* I was the first female to cross the finish line (3:45:18). I won the race for them!

---

* *After her deployment to Afghanistan, Sergeant Jill Stevens was named Miss Utah, 2007.*

PERSISTENCE, MIRACLES, AND ETERNAL RELATIONSHIPS

Chief Warrant Officer 5 Layne S. Pace
Utah Army National Guard
Afghanistan, 2003–2005

Prior to being deployed in Afghanistan, I was seriously considering retirement. I had served for many years, and my wife and I felt I had spent enough time away from home. I made the arrangements and handed in my intent-to-retire papers to my commander. He looked at the papers and then at me. Before he could say anything I reached out, took the papers back, and said, "I'll let you know when you can have that." For some reason, I knew I still had work to do in the military. I was soon thereafter deployed with my Utah National Guard unit to Afghanistan. Even though I was being sent over as a Apache helicopter pilot, I knew that there was another reason I was going. I knew there was something else for me to accomplish in Afghanistan.

After our arrival in Bagram Air Base in north-central Afghanistan, our unit developed a unique relationship with the Egyptian military personnel who ran the Egyptian military hospital on the base. The Egyptian and Korean hospitals were the only sources the Afghanistan people had for medical treatment. Our soldiers routinely visited these hospitals, taking boxes of coats, shoes, clothing, and hygiene items our families had shipped over through the

Chief Warrant Officer 5 Layne S. Pace

U.S. mail. The local Afghanis were overjoyed when we handed out these items through both hospitals.

I desired to assist Afghan villagers on a larger scale. Through persistence and a series of true miracles, I received permission for my unit to "adopt" two orphanages and two remote villages. Both orphanages and villages had numerous girls and boys. Family members in Utah shipped large quantities of goods, which we loaded in trucks and drove to the orphanages. There we handed out coats, shoes, clothing, and various humanitarian items. We also flew humanitarian items to the villages of Jegdalek and Mohammaday. The villagers thanked us profusely every time we made a trip. We also received many expressions from them about how grateful they were that America provided them with protection. They said, "We would still be under the bondage of the Taliban if America did not help."

Whenever we flew aid to these villages, it affected us deeply to see children without shoes and coats in the wintertime. On our first trip to one of the villages, it also became painfully obvious that the villagers were suffering from medical tragedies of every category. They lined up with their sons, daughters, fathers, and brothers (but never with their wives) and asked us for help with one medical emergency after another. We reminded them that we were helicopter pilots and not medical personnel. They still lined up and unceasingly asked for help.

As I reviewed digital photos I took during one recent mission, a certain picture caught my eye. It was of a little girl with her eyes crossed. I studied her face and eyes and had the impression that I might be able to help her condition. I printed the photo and took it to Dr. Gobram, an Egyptian ophthalmologist who recognized the problem to be strabismus, a muscular disorder that prevents accurate focusing. If left untreated, her crossed eyes and resulting blurred sight would become permanent. We made surgical arrangements and scheduled our next trip to this village in one week to pick the girl up. The U.S. hospital generally does not treat Afghani locals. But with some determined persuasion on our part, it agreed to assist Dr. Gobram with the eye surgery. On our next trip we showed the village elders a picture of the young girl and asked if we could take her with us. We did not know what their reaction would be. We found a very gleeful father bringing his daughter in her "best" clothing for their CH47 (Chinook) ride back to Bagram. We then learned that this precious girl's name was Halima. She was eight years old.

Prior to surgery, Halima needed to be cleaned up, so we took her to the on-base beauty salon operated by Russian women. All we asked them to do was wash her hair. They not only washed, curled, and styled her hair, but they also washed her feet, cleaned her shoes, gave her a pedicure, painted her toenails with flowers, and manicured and painted her fingernails. Considering the violent history between Afghans and Russians, this tender sight was truly amazing to behold. The women would not accept any money, so we gave them generous tips. Halima's face glowed with a nonstop smile.

A few hours after the surgery, we learned it had been a success. Her father woke her up, and she sat up with her unbandaged eyes closed. When she heard our voices, she squinted her eyes open and burst into a huge smile. This was our first hint that she could see. After one day of recovery, Halima was already seeing well, alert and ready to explore. Soldiers treated Halima and her father to lunch and dinner every day, including trips to the chow

Left: Layne Pace discovered Halima and noticed her condition from this photograph. He showed this photo to doctors, who recognized a treatable condition.

Right: Wearing a new dress and a large smile, Halima rejoices after her successful eye surgery.

hall and the on-base Burger King. During her recovery, she watched all the Disney movies we had at our aviation chapel.

As the weeks and months went by, every time I visited her village this little girl broke ranks through the other girls, boys, men, and fathers and into the midst of the soldiers, taking turns holding our hands. Without words, this innocent child showed us her loving gratitude. During several of our visits, she would never leave my side.

Ultimately we were able to provide surgical aid to about ten other children. We also helped save the leg of one adult after the Taliban attempted to kill him by rolling a large boulder over him. One of the children we helped was a twelve-year-old boy who had never been able to simply run and play. When we first met Asadullah, a nickel-sized hole in his heart prevented him from running more than a few steps at a time. His skin was tinted blue. He was always hunkered over, trying to catch his breath. He would collapse on us. An army cardiologist diagnosed his heart defect to be VST (ventricle septal defect) and estimated he had only a few years to live. This problem required delicate heart surgery using advanced medical equipment, neither of which is available in Afghanistan.

I didn't have a clue how we could help. But I had to begin somewhere, so I started emailing family and friends back home in Utah, seeking donated skills and money. This simple effort began a series of many miracles. My request made its way to a support group called AnySoldier.Com and was read by Chad and Shelby Everett (who are well-known actors from California). Chad Everett contacted Dr. Leonard L. Bailey (the famous doctor who implanted a baboon heart into Baby Fay). Dr. Bailey agreed to do the surgery and contacted Loma Linda Children's Hospital, which also agreed to provide the facility for the surgery. Another letter found its way to JetBlue airlines, who contacted us and said they would like to fly Asadullah from New York to Loma Linda, California. JetBlue also contacted Pakistani Airlines and worked out free airfare from Islamabad, Pakistan, to New York. All of this, along with procuring the necessary travel visas and passports, took place in about ten days!

On February 4, 2005, a medical team led by Dr. Bailey successfully repaired the hole in Asadullah's heart. The hospital and other charitable groups provided for the boy's remaining expenses, as well as those of his father. After two months, Asadullah returned to his native Afghanistan, where he rejoined his mother and eight siblings.

On our last visit to the village, we said our heartfelt good-byes and boarded the CH47s for our last trip back to Bagram. As our helicopters began to lift off the ground, we looked out the windows and truly could not believe our eyes. We saw our friends in an Islamic community honoring us by flying an American flag!

These experiences have changed me and several of those with whom I served. Although we have since come home from our tours in Afghanistan, several of us are now working with Afghan locals to build an orphanage and school with capacity for a thousand children. To raise funds for this worthy cause, we created an organization called The Afghanistan Orphanage

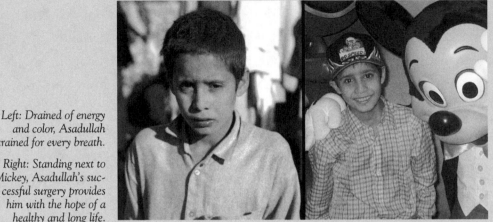

Left: Drained of energy and color, Asadullah strained for every breath.

Right: Standing next to Mickey, Asadullah's successful surgery provides him with the hope of a healthy and long life.

Project (TAOProject). Land has been donated by Afghanistan President Karzai, and building plans are now being drafted.

I have often reflected on how and why the Lord allowed these wonderful events to transpire. It all started with our desire to assist children who had no shoes or coats. As we saw the people endure their severe medical calamities, our efforts quickly focused on offering medical attention. After our last trip, it was sadly clear to me that all our efforts could not clothe or heal everyone we came in contact with. But my understanding deepened when I realized how clothing and medical aid were used as tools to build lasting relationships. We were building relationships. I am convinced that when we have all passed on and we are on the other side, there will be a glorious reunion. The relationships we have created in this life will set the stage for mass conversions in the life to come.

THE "FOG OF WAR"

Captain Tom Beckstrand

U.S. Army Special Forces
Afghanistan, 2004

During one of the earlier elections for the transitional government of Afghanistan, I was serving as the team leader of a special forces detachment in the Oruzgan Province. Our time in the country had gone much like other deployments I had been on and would go on in the future: 90 percent boredom and 10 percent hysterics. The team's specialty was unconventional warfare. In essence, that meant that a handful of Americans would work with local forces to find and combat the Taliban. Our mission was simple: destroy any Taliban in the province in an effort to provide a stable environment in which the fledgling government could establish itself.

The Oruzgan Province is located in south-central Afghanistan at the base of the Hindu Kush Mountains; it is a remote province devoid of any substantial infrastructure and makes rural West Virginia look cosmopolitan. (I mean no offense to West Virginia.) It also happens to be the birthplace of the Taliban's leader, Mullah Omar, and the birthplace of the Taliban movement itself. The valley has always been sacred ground for the Taliban and the place where the Taliban flags began to fly once again just a couple years after they were toppled in 2001. The Taliban frequently claimed that they still controlled the valley.

Captain Tom Beckstrand in the desolate Afghan wilderness

Our team was about two-thirds of the way through our deployment and looking forward to a strong finish and being home for the holidays when our headquarters began planning how to best support the elections and ensure their success. Our recommendation was to place our team in the Cahar Cineh Valley shortly before the elections in an effort to engage Taliban forces and deny them the ability to interfere with the elections. In the weeks prior, the local government had had its own forces ambushed multiple times in the valley, and they were apprehensive about what the actual election would bring. Likewise, a conventional United States unit (as opposed to a special forces unit) that had recently located at the north end of the valley had experienced substantial casualties since they had moved in just two weeks earlier, all from bombs placed in the road or ambush. Our proposal to move into the valley was accepted and incorporated into the master plan.

This was my team's second deployment to the same area in Afghanistan, and we were familiar with the terrain and obstacles that it presented. We had made many trips into the Cahar Cineh Valley and knew that if you took a substantial force, the Taliban wouldn't fight. They'd simply pick up shovels and look like farmers. The only risk would be from bombs buried in the road—a tactic employed with increasing frequency and effectiveness. It is also a tactic that's extremely difficult to avoid.

Our plan was to take a force small enough to avoid detection and target a couple of key areas that our informants had indicated were Taliban hotbeds. We took a ten-man special-forces team and about thirty of our best Afghan militia. We would move during the night and hide during the day; our targets would be a couple of compounds located at the southern end of the valley. During the first night of the operation, we covered the distance from our firebase through the narrow pass at the southern end of the valley. As day broke, we moved into a narrow draw off the valley and hid from the other traffic using the road. Throughout the day, we contacted our informants in the area to ascertain the location of a Taliban leader known to be in the valley; one informant agreed to meet up with us and to take us to him.

We moved in the late afternoon, our plan being to attack his compound and then leave as it got dark. We would then move through the night and be at our next target before the sun rose. As we crested the hill and moved down to surround the Taliban leader's compound, we began to notice a lot of movement in the village around us. The recently vacated target compound showed signs of use as a barracks; large quantities of food and bedding were present. After we had surrounded the structure and team members began to search it, I noticed two Taliban fleeing the area. As one team member pinned them down with a machine gun, three of us moved forward to engage them. In the ensuing gunfight, one died and the other was wounded. As I was returning to the initial target, the senior enlisted man on the team, Mark, asked me to come back to my truck. When I got there, the interpreter came over and told me that he was listening to the Taliban plan their counterattack on his radio. Here's what he heard:

"Get my AK-47; I will need it for the attack tonight."

"And tell the others to get their RPGs [rocket-propelled grenades] and machine guns and come down here."

"The wind and dust are too strong; they will have no help coming."

That last remark held my attention. He was right; there was a dust storm at the time that was strong enough to prevent helicopters from flying. We would have no reinforcements and no way to evacuate any casualties. I looked around through the dust and once again noticed a substantial amount of movement occurring all around us. Five guys on a tractor, two on a motorcycle, several on foot, all converging on an outdoor market about a half mile west of us. Mark then posed a simple but very difficult question. "So, what are we doing?"

Responsibility can be daunting. In a situation where there appears to be no right answer and no source of guidance, being the one charged with making the decisions can be intimidating. What if you're wrong? What if someone for whom you're responsible gets killed? Contrary to what's in the movies, there's no voice from the past with all the answers and no guarantee of a happy ending. Just . . . "So what are we doing?" I looked towards the setting sun and told Mark that we were staying put. I figured it was better to defend from a place with which I was familiar than stumble around in the dark into an ambush trying to find someplace better.

I asked Mark and Tom, the two most senior guys on the team, to establish a defensive perimeter and made some suggestions as to how I thought it should look. I then took a moment to try to figure out how the Taliban would attack and what the outcome might be. As I looked through my binoculars at the orange "fog" that was the dust storm towards the market, my entire field of view was filled with men—men just milling about, waiting. I estimated I could see well over one hundred. Most worrisome was a series of ditches that ran from the market to the compound we had just searched, which was sixty feet away from us. I realized that men could crawl down the ditches and emerge on the other side of the compound and we wouldn't know it. It would then be possible to fire several RPGs in unison from the doors and windows of the compound, initiating an attack with little or no warning. It's how I would have done it.

As I thought through how the attack might happen and what we could do to defeat it, I realized that unless our situation changed we wouldn't all survive the night. I got on the radio and contacted our headquarters element in Kandahar. I was describing to them our situation on the ground when the satellite phone in my truck started to ring. I answered the phone and was greeted by my battalion commander. He told me that we had a satellite overhead that was seeing "some interesting things happening all around you." There was also a "high probability that the men you're looking at are the same ones we've been sent to find." He offered some encouraging words, wished me luck, and then said good-bye. He was a good man, a great commander, and I admired him. But as I put the phone down, I had never felt more alone in my entire life.

Sometimes it seems as though it's easier to deal with adversity if it's consistently difficult. The more arduous the situation, the more focused and driven one may become until resolution of the crisis is all that occupies one's mind. This was one of those times for me. But when my commander offered encouragement, I was reminded of how much I missed my home and family and how badly I wanted to return to them. After receiving that kindness, the impending sense of doom I felt was all the more pronounced. I thought of my home on the other side of the world and wondered if I would ever see it again. I had a memory of placing my bare feet on our carpet and wiggling my toes, and I remembered how good it felt. I wanted to call my mom and tell her that I loved her. The recognition of the finite nature of mortality brought with it the remembrance of things we often easily forget. I remembered how comforting it was to hold a temple recommend and to know that should this be the end, I wasn't worried about my standing with the Lord. I was thankful for the opportunity to have served a mission and the testimony that can come only through service to others; it was as a missionary that I decided that I would devote my life to service. And it was my time as a missionary that placed me on the path to military special forces and my service there.

As I was standing alone with my thoughts, looking toward the men amassing to our west, Tom came and stood next to me. Tom was in his late forties and had seen action in just about every conflict our military has participated in since the 1980s; he is also a close friend and confidant. I knew he recognized our situation for what it was: dire. When I looked over at him, he just cocked an eyebrow and shrugged. "Yeah, I know," was all I could think to say in response.

With our defense in place, we waited for the attack to begin. Not long after it got dark, a teammate on the eastern side of our perimeter spotted through a thermal sight a truck with no headlights coming toward our position. It stopped about a half mile away, and nine armed men got out and started making their way toward us. Previously, while we were waiting for the attack to begin, we had called for fixed-wing aircraft to loiter above our location in anticipation of the oncoming hostilities. They could fly above the storm. I now contacted one of those aircraft and asked him to make a strafing pass to target the nine men and the vehicle. I also asked my teammate to use our .50-caliber machine gun to ensure that both the men and the vehicle didn't get away. The aircraft and machine gun struck at the same time, destroying the target.

A moment later, our interpreter got very excited and told us that we had hit some of the men he had been listening to on the radio. He also said that the Taliban were now moving inside the surrounding buildings to avoid detection. As we thought of how to target the men hiding in the buildings without harming any civilians, we realized that one of our aircraft had a smaller 40mm cannon and a larger 105mm howitzer available for use. We came up with a plan whereby we would use the 40mm cannon to shoot the buildings we suspected the Taliban were using. It was too small to penetrate the thick mud roofs and do any damage. But it also provoked chatter on the radio when we hit one of the right buildings. Slowly and methodically, we worked our way through the market and surrounding buildings. When we identified a hiding place with the smaller cannon, we then used the larger one to destroy the building. This went on for several hours.

After listening to the Taliban plan to attack after the aircraft left, I asked the aircraft to move far enough away that it couldn't be heard on the ground. My plan was to draw the Taliban out into the open and then bring the aircraft back to target them. Just as our gunship got out of earshot, he came back on the radio to inform us that he had a malfunction and really did have to leave. Ten minutes later a B-1 bomber checked in; it flew high enough not to be heard on the ground.

The Taliban's plan called for all their remaining men to mass in the market and in some compounds 500 meters north of us. My plan was to give them thirty minutes to get there and then drop three 2000-pound bombs at those locations. I conveyed my plan back to headquarters and got a phone call shortly thereafter.

"Tom, this is the battalion operations officer."

"Yes, sir."

"The ordnance you're planning on dropping is substantial."

"Yes, sir."

" . . . Okay. . . . Well, we've plotted your location on our map and where you intend to drop, and we want you to know that you'll be in range of your own ordnance."

"Yes, sir." (Minimum safe distance for the ordnance I wanted to drop was 750 meters. With us only 500 meters away from where it would hit, all of the manuals said I could expect 10 percent casualties with my own men. As much as I wished the situation could have been different, it was what it was.)

" . . . Well. . . . Okay. . . . Good luck."

"Thank you, sir."

Thirty minutes later the bombs hit. All of us knew what was coming.

With only ten Americans on the ground, it was easy to pass along information as it came available. The Afghans with us knew to stay close to their American counterparts and to do as we did. Most of the debris from the blast passed over our heads; however, Tom sustained a slight shrapnel wound to his face. He stayed with us through the night and rode out with us just before daybreak. After our return to our firebase, he was flown down to Kandahar where he underwent some minor surgery and fully recovered.

After the attack, we left before sunrise, taking a road south from our location and traveling out through the desert, and arrived safely back at our base.

In the days after the attack, we learned from our informants in that area that between two hundred and three hundred men had gathered to attack us that night. Most were killed; this included a few notable ones that had specialized skills in explosives and communications, men we knew by name. We also learned that both of the roads we had initially planned on taking north and west had been mined and had men in ambush waiting for us. This was also true of the road we came in on. The seemingly random decision to set off to the south out through the desert took us on the only unguarded route out. Tom would later comment to me, "Someone up there does like us."

In the weeks that followed I received many congratulations for the work that my team had done. I'll always remember the battalion sergeant major's remark: "All of that activity and none of you got killed. Nice work." I felt like I was taking credit for something I didn't do.

This event was one of a series that caused the Taliban's leadership to call in from Pakistan and offer a $200,000 reward or bounty for the man who could kill me. As far as anyone in my battalion knew, it was the first time that that had happened since the war began in Afghanistan.

I know that much of what happens on the battlefield can be attributed to the "fog of war." There are countless, seemingly random events that occur, and we have little to no ability to influence their outcome. However, unlike many of the men with whom I served, I have a testimony of the gospel and an understanding of the plan of salvation. I do not believe in coincidence or good luck. It is true that accidents happen, sometimes to good people. But often-times the Lord, unnoticed, intervenes on behalf of one of his children. In my case this has happened many times. There have been times in the past when I've put on a strong performance because I prepared and worked hard to ensure my success. This was not one of those times. During this event I was at the mercy of limited information and great uncertainty. This was a time where all of the odds indicated that my team should have paid dearly for being in the wrong place at the wrong time. That we not only made it away safely but also were tremendously successful demonstrates to me that Heavenly Father is mindful of his children and their needs, even when they're far from home.

I think back often to times when I have witnessed the Lord's interven-tion not only on my behalf, but on behalf of the men for whom I was respon-sible. I feel especially indebted to the Lord for his protection of my men, men who didn't know him. While it is natural to expect the Lord's protection for obeying his commands, seeing his protection of others because it was impor-tant to me has helped me to understand his tremendous love for all of his children, as well as our responsibility for them.

My time in the service has given me an unshakable testimony, a testi-mony that has come with a price but one that I willingly paid. Besides, how do you put a price on a relationship with the Lord? The risks or hardship required to come to know the Savior seem insignificant compared to the knowledge and the happiness that I've received in return. My hope is that I'll use what I've been given in a manner that is pleasing to him.

LIVING WATER

Ray Alduenda

Police Advisor/Mentor
Afghanistan, 2006

In July 2006, after a few co-workers and I enjoyed an evening meal, we decided to drive up a nearby hill to visit the site of an old mosque in Kabul, Afghanistan. This strategic outlook was used by the Russians as an observation post when they occupied Afghanistan in the 1970s. As we approached the top of the hill, we saw young adults playing soccer on a dirt field. As the youth played their sport in a cloud of dust, smaller children contently played in the dirt nearby. The moment the children saw us approaching, they ran toward our vehicles with smiles and with hands high in the air giving us a "thumbs up" salute. The children were excited to see us because they knew all American vehicles travel with fresh water. It was a humbling experience to see how grateful these children were as we handed them bottles of pure water.

It is impossible to describe the scene with words. The water normally available to these dear children comes from a few hand-powered pumps located along the streets. Long lines gather around these highly valued pumps, despite the water's unsanitary conditions. Many of these children may never have tasted fresh water before; our water was indeed precious to them. As I handed out bottles of water to my new friends, I reflected upon how I was moments before enjoying a warm, well-cooked meal in a clean setting on a guarded compound. The contrast was extreme, and my feelings are difficult to describe.

A few weeks later, my team and I were driving back into Kabul when we noticed several children along the roadway. We stopped and gave water and candy to the children. Their innocent faces lit up with appreciation. As we continued on our journey, we saw a crippled man seated on the ground a few feet from the road. With a handmade crutch beside him, he tended to a young girl who seemed to be asleep on his lap. I asked the driver to stop, and we gave the man a bottle of water and a one dollar bill. I wish everyone in the world could have seen the expression of gratitude on his face. He looked at the water and then the dollar bill and seemed to be amazed that someone cared. Making a cultural gesture of sincere gratitude, he looked at us while he touched his heart with his right hand. As our vehicles drove away, I looked back at the man and will never forget the look on his face; he had made this mission worthwhile. It is amazing how such a simple act of humanity can have such a profound impact.

Once again I was reminded how the smallest gifts can truly bless others when freely given. Although our gift was indeed small, the impression etched on my heart will *never* be forgotten. I would not trade these experiences for the world. This good man represents Afghanistan's struggle and appreciation for the Americans here. As I reflect on these and other similar experiences, I am reminded how these poor people will someday receive far greater gifts than fresh water. In the Lord's time, they will receive the gift of living water which only he can provide.

An Afghan man expresses his gratitude for fresh water by making the cultural gesture of placing his right hand over his heart.

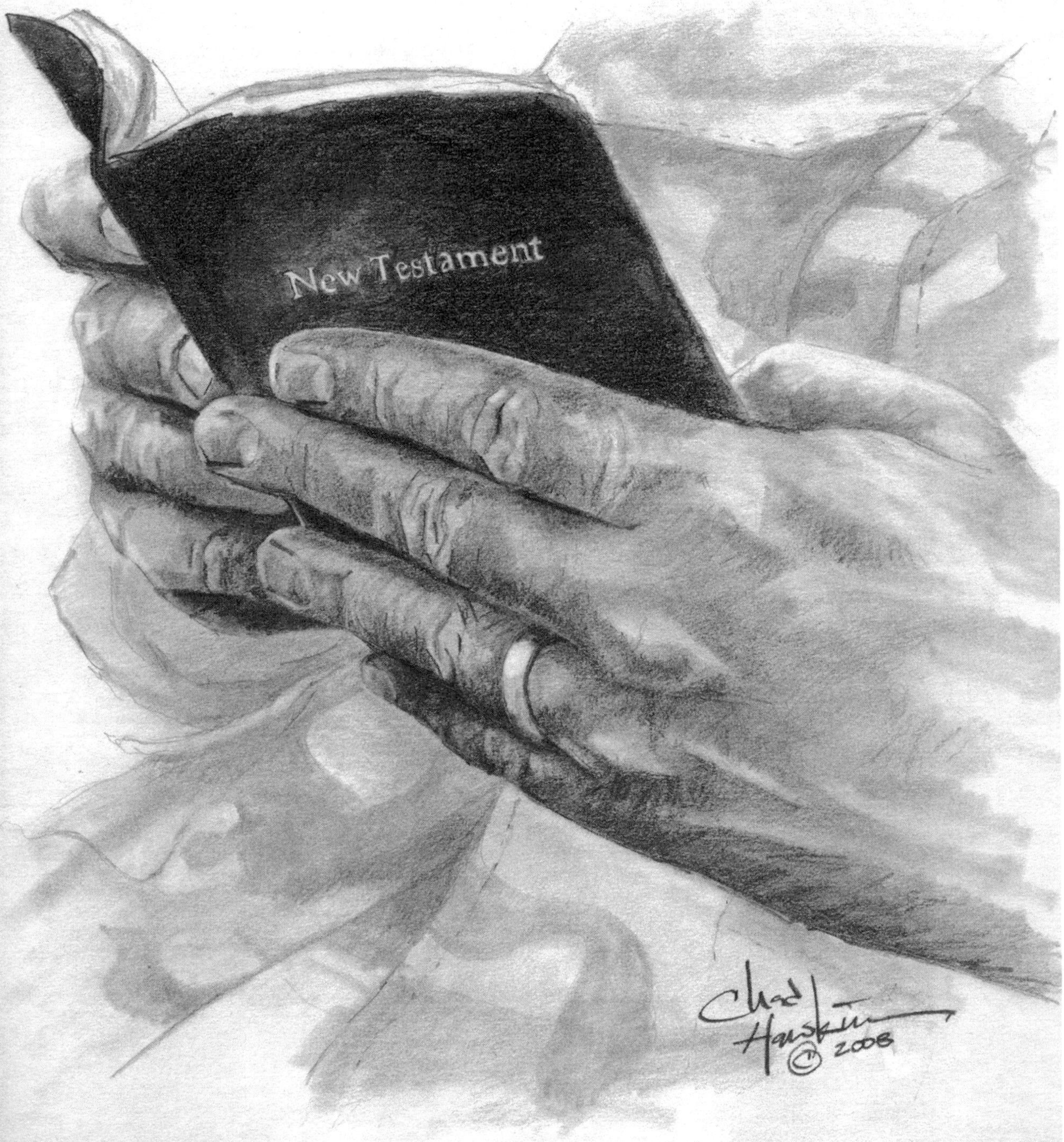
New Testament
Chad Hoskins
© 2008

LIVING *the* GOSPEL
IN DESERT FATIGUES

Freedom is not free, and securing it is not a spectator sport. You are either paying for freedom with support, sacrifice, and service, or you are free because someone else has paid the price for you.

—Chaplain Mark Allison

BULLETS FELL LIKE RAIN

*Bishop William Teuscher**
Civilian Engineer
Iraq, November 2003–February 2004

While in Iraq as a civilian engineer, I met with members of the Church in many unique circumstances. On December 14, 2003, I gathered in a tent with members of the LDS servicemen's group to observe the Sabbath. The spirit of the meeting changed from edification to confusion when bullets started to fall like rain, peppering and sometimes even puncturing the roof of the tent. The sound of spent, earthbound slugs striking the roof made for unsettling worship.

As William Teuscher labored to restore electricity, Blackhawk helicopters always seemed to be flying over.

The Coalition Provincial Authority building. Members gathered for sacrament meeting in the alcove on the day Saddam Hussein was captured.

We soon learned the source of the excitement. During our church service, news of the capture of Saddam Hussein had reached the streets of Baghdad. Following local tradition, Iraqis rushed into the streets and celebrated by firing weapons into the air. Of course, once bullets go up they have to come back down. As we were sitting there, the bullets started coming down through the tent, and we knew we had to get out.

We quickly went to the only place we could find—an open-air bowery. Our group of about twenty people was visible to everyone walking by. Tanks and armored personnel carriers rumbled nearby. Helicopters whirred overhead—and Iraqis were still shooting into the air. It was the least reverent place imaginable. It was also one of the spiritual highlights during my time in Iraq.

Despite our environment, we proceeded as best we could. We opened our meeting singing a Christmas carol, followed by an opening prayer. We then partook of the sacrament. We then sang a closing carol and said a benediction. That was our sacrament meeting. I will never forget the spirit that was there. I will never forget it—it was just wonderful.

---

* *While serving as the bishop of the Cottage Grove Second Ward in the Eugene Oregon West Stake, William Teuscher was deployed to Iraq as a civilian engineer attached to the Army Corps of Engineers. During his four-month deployment, he was not released as bishop. The ward functioned under the direction of the stake president with assistance provided by stake high councilors.*

WORSHIPPING IN HUSSEIN'S PALACE

Bishop William Teuscher
Civilian Engineer
Iraq, November 2003–February 2004

The opulent palaces built for Saddam Hussein form a stark contrast to the third-world living conditions that define the lives of most Iraqi people. Hussein's presidential compounds contained grandiose mansions, luxurious guest villas, vast office complexes, and multiple garages. Enormous sums of money went into creating manmade lakes and waterfalls, elaborate gardens, marble rooms, and other luxuries. Once coalition forces established their authority in Iraq, many of these palaces were procured for coalition objectives.

While I was in Iraq, on several occasions I met in a Baghdad palace with a few other Saints during worship

Bishop Teuscher sits in Saddam Hussein's throne, located in the Coalition Provincial Authority building.

A new friend Bishop Teuscher made at a substation. After meeting Bishop Teuscher, this old gentleman got a weapon and said he was going to stand guard as Bishop Teuscher worked.

services. These palaces *literally* were palaces, with no expense spared on materials or workmanship. An amazing, high-domed room within the palace was designated for church services. It contained one of Saddam's gilded thrones.

I thought of our temples as I walked into this palace. I compared the palace's lavish gold crystal and marble ornamental decorations with the simple, reverent beauty of our temples, where the Spirit is present. The peace one finds in a true temple of God was certainly absent from these palaces.

I remember the first time I went to church there. I was surprised to see rugs on one side of the room. These were utilized by the many Iraqi people who said their daily prayers as required by the Islamic religion. They offered their prayers a few feet away from us while we held our sacrament meeting. Week after week it was the same—we shared the same room at the same time. We were friendly with each other and respected each other's space. Despite this unique environment, the Spirit of God was there, just as we experienced it in our sacrament meetings back home.

TRUE TO THE FAITH

Bishop William Teuscher
Civilian Engineer
Iraq, November 2003–February 2004

While I was in Iraq as a civilian engineer with the U.S. Army Corps of Engineers, I attended a very impressive political gathering. In attendance were a general, colonel, and captain from the United States military, along with a high-ranking cabinet official and twenty others from the new Iraqi government. I soon found myself in a position where I was encouraged to conform to a local tradition that was not in harmony with the Word of Wisdom. As we were sitting in a hospitality room, everyone began to be served chai, which is a black tea. Iraqi chai is akin to syrup with much sweetener. When I saw what was happening, I thought I could blend in and not be noticed. I simply left mine on the table and did not drink any. After a few minutes the host came in and began to refill the cups. He noticed that mine was still full and handed it back to me. I politely declined, amidst the stares of others. This was an awkward situation because we were encouraged to honor Iraqi local traditions. Opposing customs and lifestyles may seem offensive and thereby threaten diplomatic harmony.

The next course of refreshment was coffee. Again, a cup was placed before me and soon my cup was the only one still full. At this point, the Iraqi cabinet member felt compelled to find out what my motive was. I think he

The Iraqi Nation Ministers of Electricity, with whom Bishop Teuscher worked closely to restore electricity to the country

was on the verge of being offended because I had declined their hospitality. He looked at me and inquired, "Why are you not drinking your tea and coffee?" The room became very quiet, and all eyes were upon me.

For just a second I considered what I should say. Then I responded by asking, "Are you a religious man?" He confirmed that he was. I said, "I am a religious man too, and my religion asks me not to drink tea and coffee."

The pause that followed was one of those moments when a second seems like an hour. He thought about it for a moment and then said, "Okay, that will do."

I am grateful that the Lord helped me in that meeting—and that my hosts accepted my standards in a good spirit.

BASIM JERGIS:
A PIONEER SAINT IN A WAR ZONE

Eugene "Gene" J. Wikle
Civilian Mentor to Ministry of Defense
and Afghan National Police

Iraq, 2006–

I first met Brother Basim Jergis while serving at the U.S. embassy in Baghdad in July 2004. Brother Jergis is one of the first Iraqi members of the Church in Iraq—if not the very first. Brother Jergis shared with me his experience in joining the Church.

While living in exile in Jordan he met members of the Church through his employment. Brother Jergis speaks English and was able to converse with them. Through the efforts of the members of the Church in Jordan, he accepted the gospel of Jesus Christ and converted from the Islamic faith to The Church of Jesus Christ of Latter-day Saints. Brother Jergis is not married and is the only member of his family to become a member of the Church.

After the invasion of the United States into Iraq, Brother Jergis returned to Baghdad, Iraq. When I met him, he was working as an advisor to the Baghdad municipal government. In order for him to attend church services at the U.S. embassy, he needed to be escorted as a visitor. I was one of the few members of the Church at the U.S. embassy who had visitor escort privileges. I

Gene Wikle and Basim Jergis

accepted the assignment within our servicemen's group to escort this sweet brother each Sunday to church.

Brother Jergis risked his life to attend church each Sunday. Baghdad was not a safe place to travel through, regardless of where you were going or what you were doing. Each Sunday, he faithfully arrived at the appointed hour at the U.S. embassy gate. I would be there waiting for him. He always greeted me with a warm smile and a firm handshake. He always expressed a sense of relief when we met. He was grateful that he had safely made it to church that day.

Brother Jergis and I quickly became friends. We spent time before and after church discussing his life, my family, life in Iraq, and his growing testimony of the gospel. Basim was a man who found peace in the middle of a war zone. I knew he was happy to be a member of the Church. He was ordained a priest when he was baptized. As part of his priesthood responsibilities he was assigned each Sunday to prepare and bless the sacrament. He considered this a sacred responsibility and performed his priesthood duties with great reverence. On several occasions I had the privilege of blessing the sacrament with Basim. I could feel his spirit and love of the Lord each time he knelt to offer the sacramental prayer. What a blessing it was to serve with this pioneer saint of Iraq!

I went home on leave in August 2004. When I returned in early September, I brought with me a gift that my wife and I had purchased for this faithful brother. I presented him with his own leather-bound English editions of the Bible and triple combination. He was so excited to receive these scriptures. He had tears in his eyes as he gently rubbed his hands over the books. I knew that those scriptures would become well-worn by a man who loved the Lord and wanted to read the words of the Lord and His prophets.

When I departed Iraq in November 2004, I found leaving my brother Basim to be a difficult task. I continue to think about him with a prayer in my heart that he is safe and continues to serve the Lord in Iraq. Basim is truly a pioneer saint in a war zone.

POWER FOUND IN THE SCRIPTURES

Lieutenant Colonel Larry Goodwin
U.S. Air Force
Djibouti, Africa, 2005, and Afghanistan, 2007–

I am a lieutenant colonel in the United States Air Force, stationed at Kirtland AFB, New Mexico, and presently deployed to Kabul, Afghanistan. I am in my second deployment in two years as part of Operation Enduring Freedom. In August 2005, I deployed to Djibouti, Africa, and then in April 2007, to Kabul, Afghanistan.

During my two deployments, I have truly been blessed because of the scriptures and their wonderful teachings. As I was preparing to deploy in 2005, President Gordon B. Hinckley had just issued his challenge to us to read the Book of Mormon before the end of the year. I was facing some personal challenges at the time, and I knew I had to commit myself to President Hinckley's challenge. I didn't know what The Church of Jesus Christ of Latter-day Saints group would be like in Djibouti, but I knew I would be blessed if I read the scriptures.

When I attended my first meeting in Africa, I found I was one of three active members. We met every week and, among the three of us, would bless and strengthen each other. While there, I did complete the prophet's challenge. I was truly blessed. My mind was eased regarding my challenges, and my testimony was definitely strengthened. What a blessing!

With my deployment to Afghanistan (where I am as I write this), I was pleasantly surprised to find an active group of Saints there—eighteen to twenty on average. Attending church each Friday was a sanctuary, much like visiting the temple. When I entered the room we use as our chapel, I was able to shut out the cares of the camp for two hours. It truly is a blessing to take that break each Friday.

I knew the scriptures would be important to me again, and I took them with me. My wife and I had already committed to read one chapter a day while I was gone. We knew it would keep us close to each other and help strengthen our testimonies. A few

Lieutenant Colonel Larry Goodwin

weeks after I arrived, our home stake president challenged our ward to read the scriptures and personalize each chapter to our lives. He also challenged us to write down in a scripture journal what we discovered each day as we read. I have done that every day. I also take the time each week to write an email to my wife and share my views on a chapter I read that week.

As I have followed the counsel of the prophet, a wise stake president, and bishop, the scriptures have truly blessed my life. They have truly come to life as I've applied their teachings to my life. During these two deployments I have learned that it's not enough to simply live the gospel—I must live the gospel with all my heart, might, mind, and strength, and with a total commitment to Heavenly Father's work.

Deployments can be tough. I've seen fellow soldiers, sailors, airmen, and marines affected in many negative ways. Most don't look at a deployment as a time to improve, especially to spiritually improve their lives. But I've been blessed to experience the love of the members of the Church both in Djibouti and Afghanistan. That love, which is found wherever a group of Saints meet, is wonderful to feel. Most of all, the scriptures have blessed my life. As President Hinckley stated in August 2005, "Without reservation I promise you that if each of you will observe this simple program, regardless of how many times you previously may have read the Book of Mormon, there will come into your lives and into your homes an added measure of the Spirit of the Lord, a strengthened resolution to walk in obedience to His commandments, and a stronger testimony of the living reality of the Son of God."

I can testify that the challenge of President Hinckley brings the promised blessings. The scriptures, specifically the Book of Mormon, have helped me rediscover the gospel and reignite my testimony. I know that the scriptures can point us toward the answers to all our problems. Making them personal to me has helped strengthen my dedication to the gospel.

MY FEAR WAS GONE

Lieutenant Legena Briest
U.S. Army
Afghanistan, 2007–

Before coming to Afghanistan I had a lot of fear about the prospect of such an assignment. I had wanted to get out of the military the year before because I knew I would be sent to Afghanistan or Iraq if I stayed in. My husband talked me into staying in—and it almost ruined our marriage.

When I first arrived in Afghanistan, I was terrified of traveling outside of the safety of the camp's perimeter. My first ride from Bagram Air Base to Camp Eggers was almost unbearable. All I could think of was how my nephew had been very seriously injured in Iraq two years before. I did not want to end up that way because I did not want my kids to grow up with a mom who was unable to fully participate in their lives. I did not want to be injured to the point where I could not hold my kids. I certainly did not want to die.

Although laden with anxiety, I had come to the understanding that it was right that I should be in Afghanistan. I was just not sure how I was going to be able to handle the fear. I have to travel outside the wire several times a week, and I could not allow the men that I am stationed with to see my fear, because that could affect them and how they perform. My feelings were becoming more and more difficult to hide.

Lieutenant Legena Briest in the countryside of Afghanistan

I prayed really hard those first few weeks. Not for God to protect me, but for God to take away the fear. After one particularly hard day, I went back to the barracks and cried myself to sleep, begging God to help me. I believe that God knew I was at my breaking point. I woke up the next day, and the fear was gone. I don't mean it was just easier to deal with—*it was gone!* I felt God tell me, "When I am ready for you I will take you. For now, you need to be here and you need to focus on all the good things you can do for the people here." I know I am here to help these people.

I have been here for five months now, and I am a changed person. I have traveled all over Afghanistan (the nice and not-so-nice areas). I have been blessed to meet many wonderful people and see beautiful places. I did not think I could survive this—and yet it has been the best experience of my entire life. I have especially been blessed with the gift of knowing that God is with me and that I am now an instrument for him to use. I will never question where or why I am put somewhere again.

PRAYERS, SCRIPTURES, AND PROTECTION

Staff Sergeant Benjamin Finch
U.S. Air Force
Iraq, March–July 2003;
Kuwait, September 2005–May 2006

My first month in Kirkuk, Iraq, I was unable to locate any members of the Church on my base. I asked several chaplains if there were LDS services and they either did not know or did not want to tell me. I finally found a notice listing the meeting times of various denominations, and among them was an LDS meeting schedule. The group consisted of nine brothers. We organized the chairs in a circle and held small but very powerful meetings. Even though there were only nine of us, each of us was there because we had a testimony and wanted the gospel in our lives. Our close brotherhood filled a spiritual void.

Once our group leader received an email from Elder Dallin H. Oaks of the Quorum of the Twelve. Elder Oaks inquired about the needs of each individual in our group. I was very impressed with his sincere concern for each one of us.

One thing that made it even harder to be away from my wife and daughter was that we were allowed only two fifteen-minute morale calls a week. And during those fifteen minutes, you'd have other guys waiting in line behind you, so the calls were never very private. Since I was unable to confirm that all was well back home as often as I wanted to, I learned to rely on prayer. As I prayed for my family back home, I would receive a warm feeling of comfort assuring me that my loved ones would be taken care of. The blessing of those answers helped me to make it through the days. I learned to rely on those prayers and feelings of peace. I knew (and still do) that my Heavenly Father was looking out for me and my family.

During my second deployment in Iraq, I frequently traveled with convoys moving through dangerous regions. During this time President Hinckley issued the challenge for us all to complete the Book of Mormon by the end of the year. I took that challenge, and reading the Book of Mormon became a regular routine for me. If I missed my daily reading for any reason, I could tell a difference.

Reading the scriptures gave me a protection that I could feel. This protection blessed me on a long night mission as we traveled south of Baghdad. Our convoy had taken a wrong turn, leading us into a very unstable suburb of Baghdad. Our lead truck stopped the convoy without giving notice. As we waited, I saw a white, blinding light, and then little balls of fire flew across my windshield. My vehicle had stopped right next to an undiscovered IED (improvised explosive device). The device had been buried within ten feet of the passenger door of our truck. The explosion had projected a rock the size of a fist through the passenger-side window, nearly hitting my truck commander. For at least five minutes, we could hear nothing—nothing at all. After our convoy evacuated, we stopped to inspect our vehicle and found that, other than the broken window, the vehicle received only minor damage. Once we had safely arrived at our final destination, I went into my quarters, knelt down, and thanked my Heavenly Father for protecting me. It could have been so much worse.

SACRAMENT MEETING IN A BLACKHAWK

Chief Warrant Officer 2 Jared Kimber

U.S. Army, Blackhawk Pilot

Iraq, three deployments

My first deployment to Iraq came during the beginning of the war. We had been working nonstop and under incredible stress. Being witnesses to the brutalities of war began to take its toll on us. As a pilot of a medical evacuation helicopter, I never had days off and was always on call. One Sunday my unit did not have any scheduled assignments. One of the guys in the unit who was a Church member suggested that we have a sacrament meeting. Because of my duties in the war, it had been over a month since I had been able to attend any kind of church service. I was anxious for the opportunity.

We rounded up five other men and

Chief Warrant Officer 2 Jared Kimber

decided to gather around our Blackhawk helicopter. We tried to be as formal as we could under the circumstances. After a hymn and a prayer, we placed the bread and water on the helicopter's external fuel tank and blessed the sacrament. I learned that you do not have to be in a perfect setting to feel the spirit of the sacrament.

We read from the scriptures and shared our testimonies about what a blessing it is to hold the priesthood. To bless and partake of the sacrament in such an ancient and holy land was truly amazing to us. We observed that it may have been thousands of years since priesthood holders had performed ordinances in this historic region. It was great to share that memorable experience with some wonderful guys who were trying their best to honor the priesthood—even during a war.

PHYSICAL AND SPIRITUAL ARMOR

Major Brian Crandall

U.S. Army Psychologist
Iraq, April 2005–April 2006;
Landstuhl Regional Medical Center, April 2006–

During much of my time in Iraq, I served as the group leader to our Church congregation. Our group consisted of about fifteen members, many of whom were in harm's way on dangerous missions every day. After many hours off the base, these priesthood holders would return to their quarters and begin a different type of battle. The environment most of these guys lived in was not in any way wholesome and uplifting. The other soldiers living in the same quarters would want to unwind in ways that do not meet our standards. The music, the movies, and the images on the walls were often inappropriate. It was discouraging for me to know that many of the younger members in our group were facing this degrading influence every day.

As I observed what was going on, I quickly realized that it was not the physical threat that was most dangerous to the soldiers, but it was the spiritual threat. In the army, we focus on body and vehicle armor, which are certainly important. Yet there is a spiritual armor that I believe is even more important. With the gospel, we know that if we do our best to live a righteous life and then we are shot, wounded, or even killed, we will be just fine. Life is eternal and we will be okay. However, if we are not doing what we should,

Major Brian Crandall flying out of Mosul, Iraq

if we are watching movies we should not watch, if our thoughts are not what they should be, then we have no promise. It is very easy to slip up and make mistakes by getting closer and closer to things we should stay away from.

Being fully aware of this spiritual battle, I made the "armor of God" a regular theme in our Church meetings. The soldiers in our group knew firsthand the importance of remaining focused and vigilant in danger zones. One lapse in concentration meant someone might get killed. It is the same with spiritual warfare. If we let our moral guard down in danger zones, we may die spiritually.

This theme reminds me of an experience I had on my mission in Brazil. While proselytizing we confronted a man who threatened to kill us. As he went to get his weapon, we ran away. As a young nineteen-year-old, I was really scared and shaken up by the event. We called our mission president to report what had happened, and he invited us to his home. He fed us a nice dinner and calmed us down. After dinner we watched a video on the restoration of the priesthood. Our mission president paused the video on the scene when John the Baptist was giving the priesthood to Joseph Smith and Oliver Cowdery. Our president asked, "How did John the Baptist die?" We answered, and then our president looked at the depiction of John the Baptist on the screen and asked, "How is he right now?" After a pause he concluded, "Always remember, regardless of what happens to you in this life, when you are doing the right thing you will be fine." That lesson has continued with me and became even clearer to me as I served in Iraq.

When I was in a war zone, I followed the guidelines and training I had been given by the army to keep myself safe. But more important than that, I did all I could to avoid a spiritual threat. In our Church meetings we committed to each other that when we were among comrades who use bad

Major Brian Crandall in Iraq

language or pull out bad movies or images, we would say "no" and leave. The lessons I learned in Iraq are still with me. Spiritual armor really is more important than physical armor because our spiritual armor protects us for the eternities.

THERE ARE NO EXCUSES

First Lieutenant David DeMille

U.S. Army

Afghanistan, March 2006–March 2007

Lieutenant David DeMille at a checkpoint along the Afghanistan/Pakistan border

My unit trained and assisted the Afghan border police as they sought to seal off the border between Afghanistan and Pakistan. We would visit the many border checkpoints and mentor those at each outpost. We traveled into some of the most remote areas in Afghanistan. We covered a huge geographical area, and my group of about twenty guys were basically the only U.S. forces in the area. Serving among people who know only turbulence and isolation opened my mind. The civilized world has no clue how people are living out there.

We also visited small villages to let the Afghans know that we were around and that they should report

A typical Afghani village along the Pakistan border. Lieutenant DeMille is seen with his helmet off.

any suspicious activities to us. Some of the secluded villages had never before been visited by Americans. I often considered that I was the first Latter-day Saint or priesthood holder to ever be in these outlying areas. Even though we were not allowed to overtly share the gospel, I could still share the gospel's message through actions of service. I could live with the geographic isolation from the things I love, but I did not want to be spiritually isolated, so I did everything I could to keep the Holy Ghost with me.

As we visited these areas, it was the custom of the people to invite us in to their very humble homes and offer us tea and cigarettes. My translator knew to tell them that I did not want to offend them but that I did not drink tea or smoke. They would then ask questions about my faith, and I would answer their questions. On many occasions I explained the Word of Wisdom and shared what it meant to be a Mormon. In the smallest of villages in the middle of "the sticks" in Afghanistan, Afghan citizens were being visited by a Mormon.

As far as I know, the people I met were never offended when I did not partake of their offering because it was due to my religious convictions. But I did not know that going in. The first few times I had to turn down their offerings of tea and cigarettes I was nervous, because I never really knew who was good and who was bad. There was always a chance that the offended person might want to kill me. Although we met some genuinely good people, others were sitting on the fence, and insulting them may have caused them to retaliate. As a part of their culture they will not hesitate to kill someone whom they consider an infidel. Therefore, I did not know if obeying the Word of Wisdom was going to start an incident. There was no way to know.

Nevertheless, I was determined that I would not compromise my standards. If you compromise once, it is easier to compromise the second time. There is not a different kind of gospel in a combat zone; it's all the same. There are really no excuses.

WHERE TWO OR THREE ARE GATHERED

Derek Hable

Security Official

U.S. Embassy in Kabul, Afghanistan, June 2007–June 2008

It is a comfort to be in the presence of another Church member. If I am having a bad day and I run into someone whom I know is a member, it always lifts my spirits. Being with other members makes me feel a little more connected with home and gives me a sense that I am not alone. No matter how far I get out on the front line, I can know that Heavenly Father knows who I am and is looking out for me. On many occasions after I have met strangers, we have discovered that we both are members of the Church. When that happens, we are no longer strangers; we become family. Making such a connection with Church members in a war zone in an Islamic nation is a welcome experience. Discovering a fellow member is always a gift. Where two or three are gathered . . . It is always the same regardless of where you are—and you only need two.

One time I was flying into Afghanistan and was wearing a BYU shirt. A man named Lingren was on the same flight and he noticed my shirt. We made the connection that we had both studied there and were both members. He had been in Afghanistan for six months without realizing the Church was there. He had been reading his scriptures and doing what he could do on his own. It was great to find him and bring him to Sunday services. He now meets with our congregation whenever he can.

More recently, I ran into a friend whom I knew when we were both students at BYU. He arrived here a few weeks ago and is serving on the Pakistan border. To run into him after all these years—and in Afghanistan, of all places—was truly amazing. It was great to be together again, to know that we are still members of the Church, to know that we are convinced of its truthfulness and are still dedicated to the gospel. We rejoiced at our reunion much as Alma and the sons of Mosiah did when they were reunited.

I had a special experience in meeting a brother who serves as a private security officer. We ran into each other at the embassy cafeteria. We had never met before, and yet we sat across the table and began a conversation. It did not take long before we made the connection that we both shared the same faith. Making that kind of connection forms an instant bond; it is like breathing fresh air. It meant a great deal to this brother because his duties allowed him to work only in very limited areas, and to know that he now had access to another member was very encouraging for him.

He is one of the most spiritual people I have ever met. He regularly carries multiple automatic weapons, and yet he has a very gentle spirit. As a covert security officer, he is on the street all the time. He tries to live like a local and blend in. In a very real way, he is in the world but not of the world. He is among the people. To do this he has grown a beard. Over here, people judge the size of a beard by how many fists long it is: a one-fist, two-fist, or three-fist beard. This guy had a full three-fist beard. The men he works with are former special forces servicemen and can be a morally rough crowd. Yet even though he was imbedded in an Islamic society and was working with individuals who lived a vastly different moral code, he was valiant in keeping his standards. Still, the situation was taking its toll on this brother, which caused him to go through a very difficult personal time.

This brother and I work on different compounds, so I do not see him as often as I would like. One day he emailed me requesting an immediate priesthood blessing. I seldom check my personal emails, so I was unaware of his request. Later that same day, I had business that required me to visit the other compound. I accomplished what I needed to do and went to dinner. While I was eating, the other brother walked in, noticed me, and sat down next to me. He thanked me for coming to his compound to give him a blessing. I said, "What blessing?" We quickly realized that the Lord had brought us together that evening and I was able to give this fine man the blessing he needed. The experience was a spiritual feast for both of us.

I am grateful for other members of the Church. They strengthen me, and through them the Lord has answered many of my prayers. Being with other members makes me feel more connected with spiritual things and reminds me to have an eternal perspective.

A RUSSIAN CONVERSION IN AFGHANISTAN

Henry Zander

Civilian Contractor

Iraq and Afghanistan, 2006–

Shortly after I arrived in Kabul, Afghanistan, in October 2006 at Camp Phoenix, another brother of the Church, Brother Gomez, was transferred to this same camp. Brother Gomez is from the Utah National Guard. We each independently met a young Tajik girl who worked at one of the concessionaire stores at the post exchange. Her name is Anna. Anna speaks only Russian.

During one of my conversations with her in early December (I also speak Russian), she asked where I'd worked during my life and if I'd been to Afghanistan before. I explained the many places I've both worked in and lived in, which she found very interesting. When I mentioned I had been in South Africa for two years, she asked what I did there. I explained I was a missionary there for my church. I asked if she was a Christian, and she said she was. She enjoyed and desired to engage in gospel conversations. I later asked my wife, Lori, to send me my Russian Book of Mormon from home.

Brother Gomez, who doesn't speak any Russian, had also met with her at her work and had an impression that he would like to share the gospel with her. We did not speak about our experiences until after he returned from his

R&R (rest and recuperation) in Salt Lake City with his family. While at home, he mentioned to his wife that he'd like to take a Russian Book of Mormon back to Afghanistan to give to Anna.

In January, several of us members of the Church were having dinner together in Kabul. Brother Gomez's R&R was over, and he was with us. He began to talk about his decision while in Utah to bring back a Russian Book of Mormon to give to a young lady. I immediately jumped in and said, "I know exactly who you have in mind. It's Anna!"

He said, "How did you know?"

I told him I had the same impres-

Anna and Henry prior to her baptism

sions, and I had just received my Russian Book of Mormon as well.

We discussed how to present the book to her. We faced one major obstacle: General Order #1 by the U.S. Army states that proselytizing is not allowed. Since Anna had already asked to know more about our religion through me, we agreed I would give her Brother Gomez's Book of Mormon. In the front of the book, I wrote a testimony in Russian on behalf of Brother Gomez's family and myself, and gave her the book. She began reading it very quickly and was able to easily understand it and remember what she read.

I made contact with the East Asia Area Presidency representative, who works out of New Delhi, India, and received permission for us to begin teaching her the gospel lessons. I was also able to coordinate with the Moscow

West Mission president, who quickly sent Russian lessons and reading materials; they arrived in about two weeks. Instruction began in February and progressed well. Before the lesson, though, she expressed the desire to pay tithing, be baptized, and partake of the sacrament after viewing a DVD about the Church. I was quite surprised at this quick response from her.

After completing the lessons, she said she'd like to get baptized in Russia during her vacation while visiting her father there in Ryazan. Since I was going to be in Eastern Europe at that same time, she asked if I could baptize her. I was thrilled at the opportunity. Anna Nikolayevna Davydova was baptized on Sunday, June 24, 2007, in a river near Ryazan, Russia. The small branch there was remarkably supportive. She was confirmed by the branch president, whose family had been baptized in the same location just eight years earlier.

This experience was a wonderful testimony that Heavenly Father knows and loves all his children. He brought together two brethren from different parts of the world, with one being able to speak Russian, to meet a young Tajik sister working in Afghanistan who was ready to hear about the restoration of the gospel of Jesus Christ.

I HAVE BECOME STRONGER

Kristine Stoehner

U.S. Army Corps of Engineers
Afghanistan, April–October 2007

I am a very average fifty-seven-year-old American woman currently deployed to Kabul, Afghanistan, by the U.S. Army Corps of Engineers. Even though I'm a civilian, I wear a military uniform six days a week. I work in very tight quarters and sleep in a modified shipping container known as a conex. We work long, grueling, stressful hours, a minimum of twelve hours a day, six days a week. Friday is our short day—we work four hours at the minimum. The weather here is *hot!* Being from Alaska, I sometimes dread going outside because it feels like an oven. We are required to wear our protective gear if we leave the compound, and that makes me even hotter.

By the time Friday rolls around, I am so grateful! Friday is the Islamic religious day; it is also the day for our Latter-day Saint worship services. Here in Kabul, we meet at Camp Eggers for a joint Relief Society/priesthood hour and then have sacrament meeting. Prior to church, most of us meet for lunch to become better acquainted. For members of the Church over here, these few hours are our break from the harsh reality that surrounds us. I make this time the highest priority of my life. My fellow members give me comfort, joy, a breath of fresh air, and relief from the stress and strain of my job. The talks and lessons are gifts from Heavenly Father. Each week the speakers are inspired and

Kristine Stoehner and an Afghan boy

seem to talk directly to me. I listen as I have never listened before.

I have a calling that requires me to give a brief spiritual message each week during the Relief Society/priesthood meeting. Relief Society back home is sprinkled with arts and crafts and baskets full of mementos, all supporting the lesson's theme. Here in Afghanistan, there are no arts and crafts or baskets. I try to make the lessons relevant and meaningful by including a small, unique item I hand out to the men and the few women. Instead of a basket, I use my helmet. (Many of the priesthood brothers find it funny that I pass around these items in my helmet.) The handouts have included a tiny candle to represent the light of Christ, a small flag for the Fourth of July, a toothbrush as a reminder to keep our words clean, and Snickers bars to represent the sweetness of life.

My stake president gave me a blessing before I came to Afghanistan. I was told I would become stronger, and indeed I have. I am not always a tolerant person, but being here has helped to put life into perspective. My time here has taught me how wonderful life is when kept simple. At home, I have three closets of clothes, but here I have four sets of uniforms and one set of civilian clothes. It would be nice to dress up, but where would I go? I don't need fancy dinners, twenty outfits, my huge three-story house, and an expensive car. What I do need is the gospel, my husband, the priesthood, and family.

SOLO SACRAMENT SERVICE

Douglas W. Whitney

Justice System Support Program Team Leader
Mazar-e-Sharif, Afghanistan, 2006–2007

I spent a year in Mazar-e-Sharif, Afghanistan, working with a U.S. State Department–funded Rule of Law program. With two other attorneys and an Afghan staff of five, I conducted a six-month-long training and mentoring course for ten prosecutors and twenty criminal investigators. We lived at a regional training center, which is a ten-acre tract (the same size as Temple Square) surrounded by fences, concertina wire, and concrete guard towers. When visiting the workplaces of our students, we traveled wearing body armor in armored trucks with Nepalese guards. We lived in conex containers, which are the thirty-two-foot-long steel shipping containers you see on the back of semi-trucks. These containers are divided into two nicely furnished 8' x 16' rooms, each with a bath. We were fortunate to have good Internet connection, about twenty TV channels, and a DVD player in our rooms.

It was a unique experience to be the only known Church member for several hundred miles. With the permission of Church leadership, every Friday I was able to have a solo sacrament meeting in my small room. A slice of bread from the dining facility, a little bottled water, and a white towel on a small table next to my bed served well. I was able to download some hymns

Douglas Whitney with women Afghan prosecutors outside a building made of stacked shipping containers

from the Church website for opening and sacrament songs, using my copy of the hymns in the small serviceman's *Principles of the Gospel* book to sing along. After the sacrament, I usually was able to read my priesthood and Sunday School lessons or some *Ensign* articles. It was always a treat to review the weekly message sent out via email from Brother Wikle, the group leader in Kabul. Receipt of the DVD set of the last general conference was the best of all. Those hours were a time for a spiritual recharge and a time to reflect on my testimony and my gratitude for all that our Heavenly Father has given us. Daily scripture study and prayer were ever important, so that despite the physical isolation, I never felt alone. It was an opportunity for testimony strengthening and communication with my Father in Heaven that was very real.

Spending most of every workday with the Afghan people was an enlightening experience. I came to recognize how true it is that every child of God is diligently seeking for the same truths. Our staff soon became like family to me. We were able to share in their concerns when a member of their family was ill or in danger—or their joy at the time of the birth of a child, a marriage, or an outstanding achievement by a family member. I recall a worried interpreter desperately trying to reach his family after a reported bombing incident in Kabul, and his relief when he found them to be safe. While I had to be very careful not preach the gospel, it was possible to talk with them about their Islamic beliefs and traditions and to point out the many similarities we can find in restored Christianity. The increase in mutual understanding was palpable.

We were able to set aside cultural differences for a while and to know that they love their families, freedom, and the Creator, even as we do. Some of my most precious memories are those hours-long conversations with one or more of our translators about these sacred subjects. Observing their holiday traditions of charity and compassion for the less fortunate was another important lesson for me. Their generosity despite severe poverty is exemplary for us all.

Most of our students were middle-aged men who had seen war and oppression for much of their lives. Despite that, they always possessed a bright-eyed and smiling countenance and a greeting with a customary hug and a kiss that I found touching and to which I gladly became a willing participant. Our female students were always seeking more information about family life in the United States and would spend hours looking at family pictures on my laptop. On a professional level they knew that the achievement of a free society would depend on them, and they were striving diligently to learn all they could to make that happen. They are my brothers and sisters and my friends; I will always remember them with many of the same feelings I have about the people I came to know during my mission service. I am so grateful for that opportunity.

ATTENTING THE TEMPLE BEFORE DEPLOYMENT

Lieutenant Commander Robert Horner Jr.
U.S. Navy Reserve
Afghanistan, July 2007–January 2008

Lieutenant Commander Robert Horner and daughter Elaina Mae

My wife and I were sealed in the Washington D.C. Temple. We live in Maryland and are blessed to live less than an hour away from the temple. Attending the temple has always been a joy for us as a couple and has brought us closer together. I am a convert to the Church, and serving in the temple is a highlight of my membership. My wife and I have been able to do a great deal of temple work for my family. I have also been fortunate to serve as a temple worker, which has been a tremendous strength to my testimony. It is always a spiritual experience to attend the temple.

The week before I left for Afghanistan, my wife and I spent some time in the temple. That was a very unique temple experience for me. I vividly remember leaving the celestial room and looking back, knowing I would not be able to return for a long time. That was a difficult but very meaningful moment for me. I often close my eyes and ponder that moment. To remember being in the temple is a strength to me. Since I am unable to attend the temple now, the best I can do is remain worthy of my recommend and look forward to attending as soon as I get back home.

CTR MEANS "MAKE GOOD CHOICES"

Sergeant Jill Stevens
Utah Army National Guard
Afghanistan, 2004

I treated my time in Afghanistan as a mission. I received permission to attend the Bountiful Temple just prior to my deployment. Once in Afghanistan, I tried to make my living quarters a refuge from the war and the world. To remind me of the spirit I felt in the temple, I hung pictures of the temple. Next to the temple picture was a poster featuring Captain Moroni that included the words, "If all men had been, and were, and ever would be, like unto Moroni, behold, the very powers of hell would have been shaken

Sergeant Stevens and her young friends in Jegdalek

Jill Stevens and Nijeb exchange gifts. Nijeb is holding Sergeant Stevens's CTR ring, which is attached to his necklace.

forever; yea, the devil would never have power over the hearts of the children of men" (Alma 48:17). I also wrote my favorite spiritual quotes all over my walls. My room became my spiritual sanctuary.

When I wasn't fulfilling my responsibilities as a medic, my favorite part of my deployment was my humanitarian missions. My humanitarian service became a break that I looked forward to. It removed me from the monotony of serving in the aid stations and took me among the people. Being with the locals provided me with the vision of who we were trying to serve, protect, and liberate.

We visited many villages but spent most of our time in the village of Jegdalek. During my deployment we visited the village many times and built a trusting rapport with the inhabitants. We provided them with much-needed food, clothing, and care items for their children. It was not long before we began to recognize faces and learn some names. I became particularly close to a young man named Nijeb, who was about seventeen years old. He spoke a little English and was anxious to assist us in any way he could. During my many visits, Nijeb was always my friend and gave me gifts of stones and garnishes. On our last mission, he knew he would never see me again so he asked for some kind of gift from me. Everything I had was government property and not mine to give. Then he pointed to my CTR ring. My first thought was, "No. That means a lot to me." Then I thought some more and realized how easy it would be for me to get another one. So I took it off and paused to think about how I could explain the importance of the ring. He spoke such limited English that I was not sure I could help him understand. I showed him the letters and slowly explained, "CTR means to Choose The Right." The look on his face told me that he did not understand the meaning so I tried again. "CTR means to Make Good Choices." This time my message got through. The ring did not fit on his fingers, so he attached it to his necklace. After receiving the ring, he gave me a necklace as a token of his friendship.

Leaving Jegdalek for the last time was *very* difficult for me. I had learned to love these people, especially the children. As I walked away, my little friends blew me kisses and made "I love you" signs with their hands. I can still envision looking back on these precious people as we flew away. I know we are in Afghanistan and Iraq for a reason. As the Lord has said, the gospel will sound in every ear. It may be a long time from now, but someday missionaries will share the restored gospel in these lands. When Nijeb sees the CTR ring on a missionary's finger, he will remember our friendship and listen to everything they have to say.

NFS RATED

Sergeant Jill Stevens
Utah Army National Guard
Afghanistan, 2004

Heading to Afghanistan, I knew I would be around many people who were not keeping the standards I am trying to keep for myself. That was not discouraging for me—it made me want to be true to my beliefs all the more. Although I did not want to deviate from my standards, I was not going to push my beliefs on anyone. It was amazing how after I had tried to live my life the way I should for only a few months, those around me began to be

Sergeant Stevens did her best to boost the morale of everyone she was around.

more careful about how they spoke. I first realized this when one of my medic buddies wanted to tell a story about when he was a civilian police officer. I guess he was going to share some vulgar language that the bad guy yelled out at the police. Before he began his story he looked at me and said, "Stevens, plug your ears."

From then on, those with whom I worked in our aid station had a new rating system: "NFS—Not For Stevens." This rating system actually caught on like wildfire, even moving to other departments. Whenever anyone around me was going to say something questionable, they would warn me by saying, "Hey, Stevens, this is NFS. . . . Plug your ears." It was great; I loved it. They were not making fun of me, but they were trying to help me live my beliefs. I think they respected me for trying to live my life by my standards—and for the way in which I never tried to force my standards on them. Sometimes I would walk in when a group of soldiers were watching a movie. I would ask them what they were watching and they would say, "Hey, come on in, it is FS [For Stevens]." It was wonderful that these brothers (I considered them to be my soldier brothers) would look after me that way. I was never made fun of.

One time, over forty of us were gathered in my commander's office to celebrate his birthday. Some of the officers created a "funny" memorandum to be read as a part of his celebration. As is the custom with military protocol, we all formally lined up and stood at attention to listen to the memorandum. As it was about to be read, one of the officers said, "This memo is NFS." We all started to laugh, and I knew that was my cue to leave the office. I was outside the office for nearly ten minutes listening to those inside roar with laughter as the memo was read. Afterward, someone came and invited me back in, and I took part in the rest of the festivities.

We all run into our own personal "combat zones." It may not be in a military setting, but they will come wherever you are. It is not always easy to keep one's standards and morals high, but I do know that it is *always* worth it.

CHAPLAINS *in the* SERVICE

I felt that my personal freedom was not a given I could take for granted, but something for which I was deeply indebted. One way to at least pay down some interest on this debt was to help secure for others the freedoms I enjoyed. So I joined the First Battalion of the Utah National Guard's 19th Special Forces Group as their chaplain.

—Chaplain Eric Eliason

LESSONS LEARNED ON HALLOWED GROUND

Captain Erik G. Harp
U.S. Air Force Chaplain
Intensive Care Unit, Landstuhl Regional Medical Center, Landstuhl, Germany, July 2005–

When Moses went up to Mount Sinai, he took off his shoes because the ground upon which he stood was sacred. As I serve here at the Landstuhl Regional Medical Center, I have felt many times as if I should remove my shoes as I enter the rooms of these patients. What makes the place sacred is their sacrifice. The words *sacred* and *sacrifice* are formed from the same root. To sacrifice is to make sacred. Some of these wounded warriors give the ultimate sacrifice. As I enter the room and look into the eyes of men and women who will not be alive tomorrow, who in some cases are struggling to stay alive just long enough for mom, dad, or a spouse to come so they can say good-bye, I feel I am standing on hallowed ground.

These individuals laid down their lives for principles such as freedom, liberty, duty, honor, God, and country. To me, that's sacred.

People often say to me, "How can you do it? Surely you are ready to quit after working for three years in intensive care units." I answer that this has been the most challenging yet rewarding time of my fifteen years of chaplaincy. I place my time in the ICU alongside my full-time mission in establishing defining moments in my life.

I figured something out my first year of working in the ICU. I realized that my phone will not ring and my pager will not alert me because someone wants me to join them in a birthday celebration. My presence is not requested to watch a fun movie, read the mail, or hear a good joke. When I am called, it is usually because someone is about to leave this life. Then patients, nurses, and doctors look for the chaplain. Those present ask me to pray with them, read Psalms, and provide comfort.

After assisting about thirty patients who died, I began to notice some trends. These trends have changed my whole outlook on life. One thing I've noticed is that I don't know much about the wounded individuals. The world puts emphasis on a lot of things I don't know about these people. For instance, I don't know what kind of cars they drove or what kind of houses they lived in. I don't know how much money they had in the bank or how many alphabetical fragments they had after their last names. I don't know any of that—but there are some things I do know. I know of the person's family, friends, and faith. When there is some sort of an expression of faith, hope is present. In the absence of faith, there is despair. It is always most difficult to try to comfort those who are not living a life of faith. They frantically grasp at some kind of last-minute understanding. They want me to open a passage-way that I honestly can't open for them. Sometimes they will say, "I really did not live a good life, Chaplain. I never really thought this day would come."

These experiences have changed my outlook on life. After one such experience, I went home and my eleven-year-old son, Daniel, asked me, "Dad, can we go fishing one of these days?"

At the time I was busy working on my Ph.D. in clinical psychology. I responded, "Sure we can. When I finish my doctoral program in a few years."

He said, "Dad, that is what you said when you were working on your master's degree. When will I ever go fishing with you?"

That experience with my son, combined with what I was seeing day in and day out at the hospital, had a profound impact. I realized I was spending an inordinate amount of effort on things that are not eternal in nature, things that are just not as important as they sometimes seem to be. I withdrew from that doctoral program, and Daniel and I have gone fishing quite a bit since then. After all, when all is said and done, it really comes down to family, friends, and faith.

COMFORTING THOSE WHO NEED COMFORT

Captain Erik G. Harp
U.S. Air Force Chaplain
Intensive Care Unit, Landstuhl Regional Medical Center, Landstuhl, Germany, July 2005–

I have been given a very sacred charge by the United States government and the American people to fill a unique need for our soldiers. The doctors and nurses take care of the physical needs of those who enter the hospital, and my job is to assist the soldiers with their spiritual needs. The physiologists and social workers are there to assist, but they usually use their skills in an office. Chaplains are able to serve patients at their bedside.

Here at Landstuhl, we are closer to the war zone than we are to the States. It takes only six hours for the soldiers to reach our hospital from Iraq. Often I will be sitting with the soldier as the sedation first wears off. I always address the wounded by their first names. I know their names by looking at their dog tags or medical charts. When they awake, it will often be the first alert and conscious moment since the accident or event took place. Usually they are made unconscious by a mortar attack, an IED (improvised explosive device), or RPG (rocket propelled grenade). They frequently wake up in a confused panic because they are disoriented and unsure of their environment. They often start to sweat as if they are still back in the battle. Some can talk, while some can't.

That is when I need to be there. I will say, "I am Chaplain Harp. You are in Landstuhl, Germany, and you are safe." I tell them, "We love you." I use the word "we" to represent the American people, as well as the chaplain corps. Then I tell them in a more specific way: "I love you." Sometimes those army guys will look at me funny when I say that, but soon they learn that I really do deeply care and that I don't have an agenda.

The intensive care unit is a ministry of touching. To comfort the afflicted, I will hold their hand. If they have lost a hand, I will put my hand on their shoulder. If their shoulder is bandaged, I will put my hand on their head.

Once they are aware of their situation and circumstances, they have an overwhelming desire to get back to their place of service. Countless times I've heard someone say, "I have got to get back! Fix me up so I can get back! I need to get back to Iraq!" One sentiment I often hear is, "I need to get back to my boys. Someone is doing my job because I am not there!" That is when I will remind them of their injuries. I try to speak their language by saying, "You are a good soldier. You have been given a new set of orders, which indicate you are to go back to the States. You need to be united with your family and get better. You are going to get a new sergeant and that sergeant is going to be your physical therapist and you are going to do what he says."

I am a convert to the gospel, and I am indebted to the missionaries who saved me spiritually. Therefore, I feel a driving obligation to somehow help relieve the pain of another. I do it inadequately; there are too many of them. But it gives me strength to know that this is the Savior's work. I often think of the words, "When I was sick ye came unto me. When I was in prison ye visited me." For the soldiers who come here, their bodies can be a prison. The Savior's words give me strength as I try to fulfill my duty here at the hospital.

"DEAR SOLDIER" DONATIONS

Captain Erik G. Harp
U.S. Air Force Chaplain
Intensive Care Unit, Landstuhl Regional Medical Center, Landstuhl, Germany, July 2005–

One of my responsibilities here at the hospital is to oversee about 90 percent of all the donations that come to the Landstuhl Regional Medical Center. I receive, sort, and distribute these items to the wounded warriors. I am amazed at the generosity of others. We have received $2.5 million in donations in the form of cash and goods during the last two years. With the cash we purchase comfort items like sweats, shirts, and socks.

The donations are often sent with accompanying letters. We call these letters "Dear Soldier" letters. I recently received a Dear Soldier letter written by an elderly lady. She wrote, "I am on Social Security and I do not have much money. But my prescriptions are paid for and I have already been grocery shopping this month. I am sending you a $5 bill. Please purchase something that will make your life more comfortable. Thank you for your service. God bless. Signed . . ." I read that and thought about someone's grandmother doing her part in the war effort. I am often touched most deeply by these "widow's mite" contributions because of their sincerity.

The remarkable nature of this story is deepened when the soldiers receive these items. When I present the donations I say, "Soldier, these items were

Chad Hawkins and Chaplain Harp stand in a room full of donated items to be given to wounded soldiers. As soldiers visit the Landstuhl Regional Medical Center, they are invited into the room to take any item they may need.

donated by grateful Americans to YOU!" The recipient, of course, is grateful—but often he or she will say, "Thank you, Chaplain, but surely there is a soldier worse off who needs this gift more than I do. I can't take this because I'm sure there is someone else who is in worse shape."

I then look at the soldier, who may be missing a leg and leaning on a crutch, and say, "These items were meant for YOU. Please accept them."

After accepting the items, these same soldiers will often withdraw money from their personal bank accounts and donate to the charity they just benefited from. This happens almost every day! It truly is a wonderful thing to witness.

These donations are from patriot Americans who want to make a difference by *showing* their support of the troops. Receiving these items is a constant reminder of the goodness of the people back home. Performing this rewarding duty in my ministry, I have come to understand more fully the parable of the widow's mite. I have seen firsthand how a small, yet sincere gift can have a significant impact.

"SINGLE SHOES"

Captain Erik G. Harp
U.S. Air Force Chaplain
Intensive Care Unit, Landstuhl Regional Medical Center,
Landstuhl, Germany, July 2005–

Chaplain Harp in his office holding the bin of "Single Shoes"

When I arrived at the Landstuhl Regional Medical Center, I was given the responsibility to manage the receiving, sorting, and distribution of all incoming donated items. While being briefed on my duties, I visited the large facility where the donations are stored. Along a wall of newly purchased shoes, I noticed a large bin overflowing with single shoes. Without waiting for an explanation, I said, "Why would our suppliers take advantage of us by sending so many single shoes?" One of the volunteers quickly interrupted me. In a somber tone she explained, "Chaplain Harp, the shoes in this bin are the remainders from sets of shoes. The other shoes went to soldiers who left the hospital with only one leg. Over the months, this tub has filled up."

At one time someone suggested that we get rid of all the single shoes, but our colonel suggested that we keep them as a "silent memorial."

I have since placed this bin in my office on top of my locker. The bin is made of clear plastic, and I see the shoes every day. It is hard for me to have a bad day when I can look up at this tub marked with the words, "Single Shoes." It puts into perspective my position as a chaplain and the price of freedom.

LEARNING FROM OTHER FAITHS

Captain Erik G. Harp
U.S. Air Force Chaplain
Intensive Care Unit, Landstuhl Regional Medical Center, Landstuhl, Germany, July 2005–

Most of the time when a chaplain visits a patient, the patient knows the chaplain will likely not be a member of his or her exact denomination. Patients seldom even ask what faith I am. They see the cross on my uniform, which is the symbol of a Christian chaplain, and that is sufficient. Counseling so many wounded soldiers has been enriching because I have learned from their faiths. I have learned from their prayers. As Latter-day Saints we do not have a monopoly on faith. We are not the only people who do our best to live righteous lives. The world has many devout people who love their Lord and Savior based upon their understanding of the Bible. I am amazed at how many times others have ministered to me. Although I am the one there to administer and provide comfort, I have often been the receiver.

When I leave a hospital room, patients will often say, "God bless you, Chaplain. Thank you for being here when I needed you. Thank you for coming." I have even had soldiers say, "Chaplain, I want to pray with you." They will take my hand and offer a prayer. I am there to pray for *them*, and they will pray for *me*. There they are, broken and in pain, and they will pray, "Please bless Chaplain Harp, his family, and his ministry. Bless him that he will be equal to his great task." I have been blown away by their thoughtfulness and example. Despite differing doctrinal backgrounds, the universal language of love is generally spoken, and many desire to serve a brother in need. I have often thought that if we could maintain more of that feeling in the world, we would surely be approaching Zion.

DESTROY MY ENEMY
BY MAKING HIM MY FRIEND

Captain Eric Eliason
U.S. Army Chaplain
Afghanistan, March–May 2004

As new Afghan armies are recruited and trained to maintain order in their deeply religious country, Afghan soldiers naturally begin to seek chaplain support. Religious leadership in Islamic countries is much more valued than it is in the West. So while Afghan soldiers are being trained to become professionals, training is also taking place for Afghan chaplaincies. Considering that the conflicts of the region have religious dimensions, the developing role of chaplains will have an increasing importance. As Americans, we did not want to meddle in their religious affairs, but we did need to foster chaplaincies that wouldn't succumb to radical religious leaders.

In the spring of 2004, I developed and conducted a short chaplain training program for a man named "Maseullah," the indigenous mullah (Islamic religious leader). Though our backgrounds—a militant-trained Afghan mullah and an American Christian chaplain—might make us seem unlikely friends, Maseullah and I shared an almost instant bond of purpose. I became known as "the American Mullah." That I was a Christian became of secondary importance to him. In the course of this experiment, we learned the truth

*Maseullah and Chaplain
Eliason on a hike to
Camp Blessing*

and wisdom of an old Afghan proverb that was one of the guiding lights of
our project, "I destroy my enemy by making him my friend."

Maseullah quickly put into practice, in real-world combat situations, the
training from our lessons together. I explained, "When you go to minister to
an injured person, tell them who you are and what is going on. You are a
symbol of God's love and watchfulness over soldiers."

"It's curious," Maseullah had responded, "but even my soldiers who are
not very good Muslims like seeing me. They seem more calm when I am
around."

"That's because they can see you are a peaceful person who is right with
God. This makes them feel secure. That is why they chose you as their mullah," I had said, referring to his role as his soldiers' elected pastor.

Maseullah dramatically "switched on" to the idea of promoting religious
tolerance and freedom, at great risk to himself. As my student, he was a
marked man by allies of the Taliban. He was going against the enforced prop-
aganda that America was the Great Satan. One day I met with Maseullah
after being separated from him for some time. He told me that he had been
with his prior teachers in Pakistan. He confided with them that he was

Chaplain Eliason near Nangalam

working with the Americans and said to them, "They are not the crusaders you said they were." He supported his statement by citing the many worthy actions of his American friends. They refused to believe him, so he invited them to come to witness it for themselves.

Through the eyes of Maseullah and other Afghans, I witnessed that freedom from tyranny was affecting peoples' lives. I saw refugees returning from Iran and Pakistan to their homes. I worked with members of an Afghan women's group, no longer hunted and murdered by the Taliban, now operating freely for the benefit of Afghan women. I listened to people excitedly discussing, for the first time in their lives, differing opinions about candidates in upcoming elections. I saw girls going to school for the first time. I watched independent farmers freely planting lucrative crops the Taliban had earlier monopolized for themselves.

During one of our many conversations, Maseullah said, "You see, Chaplain, whether I live or die is no matter. I will die when I die, and I hope to die while doing what is right—regardless of the dangers. It is all in God's hands. We are working together, you and I—a Muslim and a Christian working together to conquer those who don't like the idea of a Muslim and a

Christian as friends here in Afghanistan or anywhere in the world. If God wills, we will prevail; so we need not fear." I sensed a great lesson in this for both America and the Muslim world in these times of trouble. Without fear there is hope.

A BAPTISM IN UNIFORM

Major Gerald White
Utah Army National Guard Chaplain
Iraq, 2004; Afghanistan, 2006

I arrived in Iraq in June 2006. While serving on Camp Cooke in Taji, Iraq, I met a young woman U.S. soldier. Sister Hodges had recently been taught the gospel by the servicemen's group leader. She accepted the gospel and was prepared to be baptized. The base actually had a font. The font was a round, above-ground, thick cement structure. It was outdoors, and the only way to fill the font was to enlist the services of the fire department. She had to step up and over the font walls and into the water, which was about

Sister Hodges stands in her wet fatigues holding a towel moments after her baptism.

Large font in open view at Camp Cooke, where Sister Hodges was baptized

four feet deep. There was no white clothing available, so we received permission to baptize her in her army combat uniform. To see her lifted out of the font wearing fatigues was quite a sight, certainly not the norm.

Since the font was out in the open without privacy, we decided to hold the baptismal service at 6:00 A.M., when base activity was at a minimum. We held a full service with speakers and hymns. We even had a few curious nonmembers participate with us. In some respects, it was just like the baptismal services back home; in other ways, it was likely one of the most unique baptisms ever performed. It was amazing to think that Sister Hodges was baptized in the land of Abraham, Isaac, and Jacob. For her family, this story will be passed down from generation to generation and will be a blessing to her posterity.

Reflecting on the event, I often wondered why the font was there in the first place. I was told it was constructed to perform Protestant baptisms. Knowing that very few Protestant denominations perform baptisms by full immersion, I could see that the Lord was involved in this sweet sister's life from the beginning of her conversion all the way to its fulfillment through her baptism.

BEING A CHAPLAIN

Major Gerald White

Utah Army National Guard Chaplain
Iraq, 2004; Afghanistan, 2006

My wife would say that I am a much better person since I became a chaplain. Being a chaplain is like being called as a full-time missionary or as a bishop. I should *always* be doing the work of the Lord. There is a constant expectation for chaplains to be doing the right thing, in the right place, for the right reasons, regardless of time, day or night. When you are a chaplain, regardless of your denomination, eyes are *always* on you. Chaplains represent the Lord. Many whom I serve regard chaplains to be the Lord's mouthpiece and the Lord's ears.

There are many stringent requirements to become a chaplain. Perhaps the most important is to be, as the army vernacular states, "a squared-away individual, with himself and God." I have strived to live worthy of this expectation. Perhaps that is why my wife would remark on my positive change.

People tend to think that chaplains, like bishops or stake presidents, have a permanent sacred body of armor around them and that nothing ever affects them. That is not true. We are affected by the daily impacts of soldiers being injured or dying or of someone needing a shoulder to cry on. As chaplains fulfill their duties, they themselves do not have a shoulder to cry on because they *are* the shoulder. Therefore, I have learned to lean more heavily on

Heavenly Father, my Savior, and the Holy Ghost. When I serve as a full-time chaplain, I am directly influencing many lives and have learned to depend on God's direction. I do my best to ensure that I am doing his will and not my own.

Being deployed in Iraq and Afghanistan brought many truly amazing experiences. I think God gave me these duties to get me out of my comfort zone. For the first time in my life, those surrounding me did not embrace my faith. I was, in fact, surrounded by people who did not like me specifically because of my religion. When an LDS chaplain receives an assignment, it is known far and wide that he is a Latter-day Saint, even prior to his arrival. My first experience in Afghanistan was with a colonel whose first words to me were, "I don't want you here and I don't need you here. I already have an LDS chaplain. Why do I need you?"

It was a rough start. I worked hard to prove that I could be a chaplain to all the soldiers, regardless of their faith. When I began serving my congregation, I had six members. Within five months, over thirty people of different denominations attended regularly. My colonel and I ended up having a strong working relationship; he even gave me a very positive evaluation report.

The beginning of my next responsibility also had a rocky start. When I arrived on my assigned base in Iraq, I was told by a soldier, "You are an LDS chaplain, and we are not going to come to your services. I do not see how you can be true to your faith and still conduct Protestant services." I met with this individual many times, and he was surprised to learn of our many common beliefs. I said to him, "I'll make you a promise. If you do not like the way I conduct services, I will personally escort you to whatever service you want to go to." He agreed to my deal and ended up attending my meetings during my entire stay. I had to earn his trust by demonstrating I could preach true sermons according to the gospel of Jesus Christ without introducing doctrines unique to the LDS faith.

Another important part of my duty as a chaplain is to provide words of counsel and comfort. I have learned that one of the best ways to counsel others is simply to listen. I always try to let the individual with whom I am counseling do most of the talking.

Soldiers come to me because they know they are safe in doing so. Whatever they tell me stays with me. I am not a threat to anyone because I do not have any influence over their careers. Chaplains hold a rank but they do not write evaluations.

When I do offer words of counsel, I do my best to allow my words to be directed by the Spirit. I remember an instance when I was called to the hospital on Bagram Air Base. The airman I was visiting had sustained massive injuries to his legs. I had been in the country for only two days. I did not know anything about this soldier, so I was not sure what to say. I introduced myself to him and asked him how he was doing. Although he was in a lot of pain, he shared with me that since his wife was a Catholic, he thought of himself as somewhat of a Catholic. We prayed together, and I asked him if he would like a copy of the scriptures, to which he agreed. I went back to my office and retrieved the scriptures. As I did so, I was inspired to think of a verse in Joshua. Joshua 1:9 states, "Have not I commanded thee? Be strong and of a good courage; be not afraid, neither be thou dismayed: for the Lord thy God is with thee whithersoever thou goest."

I highlighted that verse and gave him the Bible. He was then evacuated out of the country. I never saw the soldier again, nor do I know why I was prompted to share that verse with him. That is one of the many examples in which I followed the Spirit and then left the rest in the Lord's hands.

A TRIP OF MIRACLES

Major Gerald White

Utah Army National Guard Chaplain
Iraq, 2004; Afghanistan, 2006

During the first week of June 2004, I was approached by a soldier and asked if I would travel with his convoy. The convoy was leaving Bagram and heading to Asadabad through Jalalabad, a distance of about two hundred kilometers. I agreed because it was an opportunity to ride and minister to soldiers moving through the country of Afghanistan. The convoy left mid-morning and headed out the gate, fully loaded with all of our gear and an enthusiasm to get to Asadabad. Little did I know the trip was going to be an *all*-day long adventure. The roads were dusty and dirty, with little pavement except from Bagram to Kabul. Once we left the Kabul area the roads turned to dirt, washboard style. We drove for several hours, traveling no faster than thirty miles an hour. Our convoy had a few armed vehicles, along with several trucks needing protection.

At about 1300 hours, we stopped along the road to stretch. Soldiers jumped out of the vehicles and set up a perimeter in case of an ambush. As we prepared to leave, our lead vehicle wouldn't start. A mechanic ran to the lead vehicle to analyze the problem. The bolt to the starter had dropped out, paralyzing the vehicle. Although we thought we would never find the bolt, we located it on the ground right where the vehicle had stopped.

During our return from Asadabad, we were driving in a light sandstorm; vehicles could be seen only two or three car lengths away. It reminded me of a very hazy, smoggy day anywhere in the United States. Ahead of us was "ambush alley," a long stretch of dirt road with a slight rise in elevation on each side. Strategically, it was a perfect place to be attacked, and many ambushes and fatalities had occurred there. As we entered ambush alley, our left rear tire blew out. We were forced to stop right in the middle of this dangerous location. Again, soldiers jumped out of the vehicles and set up a security perimeter. Our safety was compromised and our nerves were on edge. As the tire was being changed, the sandstorm rapidly increased in intensity. Everything around us became invisible as more and more sand was tossed in the air. My vehicle commander asked if I was praying. I said, "I haven't stopped since we left Bagram."

After the tire was changed, the vehicle was lowered—and to our shock, the spare tire was flat. With a flat tire, we had to travel through ambush alley at a pace of only one or two miles an hour. The fierce storm forced us to remain close together. We had no idea if the enemy was near.

After inching along for eight miles we saw a lighted sign. Lighted signs in the countryside are relatively rare in Afghanistan because most small villages usually don't have electricity. But there was that lighted sign. We pulled in and, using very basic English, asked if anyone had an air tank. Filled with gratitude, we inflated the tire. As we pulled out of the gas station the blinding storm subsided.

Our adventure continued as we began to climb a very steep pass. The vertical climb caused the second vehicle in the convoy to overheat. We all stopped as the mechanic inspected the problem. He told the convoy commander that we should proceed but predicted we would soon have to tow the vehicle back to base. Towing a vehicle uphill in a combat zone one hundred miles from base was a worst-case scenario. I remember saying a quick prayer asking for help to get back safely. We proceeded up the mountain into Kabul and, thankfully, arrived at our distant base without having to tow.

I am convinced we were watched over and protected throughout our long journey. Finding an essential, lost bolt; experiencing a blinding sand-storm that shielded us from the enemy as we drove through ambush alley; seeing a lit sign in a place where electricity is scarce; and being able to drive a disabled vehicle to its destination—to me, all these are miracles. I am not sure why we were so blessed, but I am very grateful we were.

A SOLDIER'S CHAPLAIN

Major Henry D. McCain
U.S. Army Chaplain
Iraq, February 2004–January 2005;
March 2007–February 2008

I received a revelation in the temple prior to my first deployment. In the temple the Lord told me that my life would be spared and that I would return home. That revelation has stayed with me and provided me great comfort for the last five years. Although I might be injured, I know I will still go home to my family. When I arrived in Iraq, the U.S. Army thought the country was more secure than it actually was. Most military authorities thought the active combat phase of the war was approaching its end and that a rebuilding phase was about to begin. That was not the case. The well-enforced Maudi Army began another period of resistance.

After acclimating myself to the region, the war, and my duties, I determined it was important for me to travel with the soldiers outside the wire. I wanted to experience what the soldiers were experiencing. I knew I could be a better chaplain if I could fully relate to the life of my soldiers. Chaplains are officially ordered to be "noncombatants," which means we do not carry a deadly weapon at any time. So every time I travel outside the wire I am provided a chaplain's assistant, who serves as my bodyguard.

Since I am among my men, they are more willing to come to me. They

162

Chaplain McCain leads a group of soldiers in prayer prior to going "outside the wire."

know I understand the heat, combat stress, and shock and grief of casualties. Putting your life on the line with the soldiers earns respect in a way that nothing else can. A lot of guys hesitate to visit me openly, but they will knock on my door late at night to unload some of their concerns. They will say, "I need to talk, Chaplain. I know you know what it is like to be shot at. You know what it is like to lay your life on the line, and I am having some issues with these things."

For these reasons, I felt like I really *had* to go outside the wire with them. Being with the men also helps me understand their morale and know when they are being pushed beyond their limits.

Chaplains are blessed from God with the ability to be sufficiently strong for themselves and their flock. Personally, I maintain my spiritual strength by reading the scriptures, praying with real intent, and seeking to be sanctified by the Lord. I seek after him and pray for his Spirit to be my constant guide. In addition, I feel it is very important to be well rested. At night I am able to sleep because I say my prayers and leave my burdens at the altar of the Lord. The next day I am refreshed for my soldiers. Sometimes this work becomes too much for me to bear alone. Then the Lord sends someone to whom I can bare my soul. Sometimes that person is another Church member; other times it has been a fellow chaplain. These people help me along this difficult ride and help me get back to a higher spiritual and emotional level.

Once I had a special experience as I was getting into a vehicle to go out on an early-morning patrol. As I climbed into the vehicle, one of the soldiers said, "I had a dream about you last night. I was in a building that was surrounded by the enemy, and it didn't look like we were going to get out of there alive. I said a prayer and you showed up. Chaplain, when you walked up the stairs, I knew we were going to be safe."

I was deeply touched by his words. I knew then that going out on patrol with my men was paying off. I knew that it was paying off to knock on their doors at night, go to chow with them, and just talk with them when they were simply sitting outside. When I go on patrol with them, we're together all day long. Some days those patrols can be very boring. In a period of eight to twelve hours, there is a lot of time for conversation, questions, and stories.

Some of the soldiers know that although I have been in a dozen attacks, I have remained safe—and no one with me has ever been killed. On three separate occasions, my vehicle has been directly hit by the blast of an IED and no one suffered injuries (except for losing their hearing for a day or two). Word spread around the battalion that God was protecting his chaplain. As I go out on patrol, soldiers sometimes fight over which vehicle I should ride in. They like the chaplain around them because they believe God is protecting him—and they too will thereby be protected.

I went out on patrol among the farmlands outside Baghdad. We had been told that the area didn't pose much of a threat. Our team leader had recently returned to us after recovering from being shot three times. He had three months left on his tour and rather than go home, he chose to come back and finish out his duty in Iraq. We were driving back and forth along the same country road. All along we were intently looking out the windows for IEDs because we know that they are so easy to plant and disguise. I was in the last vehicle of our three-vehicle convoy.

Suddenly there was a blast outside the passenger door. Our vehicle was immediately enshrouded by smoke, dirt, and rocks. At that moment my mind was racing. I thought, "My gunner—is he alive? Have I been hit and I am not feeling it yet?" The vehicle was filled with smoke, and I couldn't see or hear anything. I couldn't even feel myself to know whether or not I was hurt. We drove on and as the vehicle cleared, I prayed that everyone would survive the blast. Sure enough, with the smoke and dust gone, all reported that they were fine. One of the soldiers looked right at me. I could see his thoughts in his eyes: "Thank God the chaplain was in our vehicle today!" We determined that the IED had been buried too deep and we had been hit by the top soil and not the weapon itself.

Of course, a chaplain has many different duties. A chaplain can be called upon at any time to provide comfort and counsel, or to give a blessing. I may get word day or night that a soldier has been killed, and I will jump in a vehicle and head in his direction. I might receive a Red Cross message in the middle of the night informing me that a soldier's father or mother has died. Within moments of receiving the news, I am heading towards the solder's quarters. I am praying the entire way to know what the Lord would have me say as I break the news. Being a chaplain is similar to serving a full-time mission. I never know what the next day may bring, so I need to always be spiritually vigilant.

THE ARMOR OF GOD

Major Henry D. McCain
U.S. Army Chaplain
Iraq, February 2004–January 2005;
March 2007–February 2008

Putting on the armor of God is a message I preach to the soldiers. Out here it is a very real thing, and it provides us great inner peace. I have handed out Armor of God coins that many of the soldiers keep with them at all times. These custom-made coins visually illustrate the scriptural passage found in Ephesians 6:11–18. Some feel the coin in their pocket and remember what

Chaplain McCain standing between two other chaplains

it means. Some keep it on their nightstand as they sleep. It reminds us that God is the source of our real strength and protection.

One of the dangers of serving in a war zone is that some people think they don't need to read their scriptures or say their prayers. Too often people of many different denominations come here and take a spiritual vacation. When they go back home, they leave as hollow and empty as if they never had the gospel in the first place.

The same thing can happen in the everyday lives of people back home. People living back home need the armor of God just as much as we do in a war zone. Temptations are out there, and people need their armor on. If Satan can't kill you physically, he will try to kill you spiritually. When members start to become complacent about their prayers, scripture reading, and going to the temple, they take off their armor and become a casualty of spiritual warfare.

POWER OF THE PRIESTHOOD

Major Henry D. McCain
U.S. Army Chaplain
Iraq, February 2004–January 2005;
March 2007–February 2008

The main military hospital located in Baghdad is the Combat Army Surgical Hospital (CASH). It is located in "The Green Zone" which is a well-fortified, secure area where high-ranking U.S. and Iraqi officials are located. As soldiers are wounded they are driven or flown to the CASH, where they are stabilized and prepared to be flown to the large military hospital in Landstuhl, Germany. For the first three months of my deployment, I visited wounded soldiers at the CASH every three days.

When I arrived at the hospital, I would immediately start looking for my soldier among rooms that contained three or four recuperating soldiers each. When I found my soldier he would often say, "Chaplain, I *want* a blessing; I *need* a blessing; *please* give me a blessing." Nearly every time I performed a priesthood blessing, the other soldiers of different faiths in the room would each ask, "I know you are not my chaplain and are busy, but would you please give me a blessing too?" I would go around the room one at a time giving blessings of mental, physical, and spiritual healing. On many occasions I would use up the *entire* bottle of oil in one hospital visit. I have felt the healing power of the Lord go through my body and into theirs. To my knowledge the soldiers recovered to an extent they never thought possible. If their ability to walk again was in question, they were able to walk again. If they were worried about a large scar, the scar healed and was barely noticeable. If their extremities were damaged, they were able to function again. Those soldiers had faith in the blessings, and the subsequent healing was due to their faith as much as mine.

I had the opportunity to provide a priesthood blessing for a wounded Iraqi female interpreter. We had worked together for some time and had developed a good friendship. I visited her and asked, "I know you are a Christian with Islamic background, would you like a priesthood blessing in the tradition of my faith?" She agreed and in the presence of several others, I laid my hands on her head and gave her a blessing of healing and direction. A few weeks later she was up and fulfilling her duties as a translator.

I had a very unique opportunity to confer the Melchizedek Priesthood on an Iraqi member. This good brother attended church with the Saints on base on a regular basis. He traveled on very dangerous roads every Sunday. I then met him at the gate and escorted him on post to attend our meetings. He had been a faithful member for a long time and asked me to confer upon him the Melchizedek Priesthood. After receiving permission from Church authorities, I ordained this brother to the office of an elder. I was prompted to tell him that he would see wonderful changes in his country and would have many opportunities to use the priesthood within his own family. Standing in the circle with me as I ordained this brother was a son of a member of the Quorum of the Twelve Apostles. It was an inspiration to Church members here to know that the Apostles cared about us, knew about us, and had their own sons serving in the military here in Iraq.

THE HOPE OF A RESURRECTION ON EASTER

Major Henry D. McCain
U.S. Army Chaplain
Iraq, February 2004–January 2005;
March 2007–February 2008

It was early Easter morning in 2004, and we had just had an uplifting Protestant service. Following the service, at about 10:00 A.M., we received word that an Apache helicopter had been shot down. We did not yet know of the status of those in the helicopter, but we knew we had to get to them. They had crashed off post in an unsafe area during an intense time of the war. The military had ordered that no one was allowed off base unless it was an emergency mission. This was an emergency, but as we proceeded out the gate I remember someone saying, "You are all going to die. It is too dangerous for you to go out there."

As our convoy proceeded, we passed other convoys—each one burning and abandoned. We could feel the insurgents roaming the countryside. Once we located the chopper we began to secure the area. As we were getting out of our vehicles, two Iraqi insurgents jumped out of a canal and started raining fire down on our vehicles. We returned fire, and they disappeared back into the canal. I was then told that a chaplain had previously come by and did an open prayer for the deceased soldiers. The previous chaplain did not know who the deceased were but he did pray for them. I wanted to know who the soldiers were and pay them the proper respects, so I ran to the chopper. It was still on fire, so all I could do was grab the dog tags off the pilot and an I.D. bag from the other. I now had their names. My commanding officer was a Catholic, and he instructed me to perform their last rites. I was able to offer the appropriate prayer using their names: Colton and Fortenberry. I will never forget those names. These pilots had been shot down while trying to save other U.S. soldiers in a convoy.

As I offered their last rites, I was thinking that it was Easter morning back home in the States. If these soldiers had children, their children were perhaps looking for their Easter eggs. I thought about the meaning and importance of Easter, the miracle of the Savior's resurrection, and the incredible hope and promise that resurrection provides us all. Even though these two heroes had died, they will someday be resurrected and restored whole, with perfect, immortal bodies. I look forward to the day when I will meet them as resurrected beings. This life is only a temporary state—but because of the miracle of our Savior's resurrection, we *will* all be restored 100 percent.

"GOOD TIDINGS . . . TO ALL PEOPLE"

Major Mark L. Allison

U.S. Army Chaplain

Afghanistan, January 2004–April 2005

"And the angel said . . . I bring you good tidings of great joy, which shall be to *all people*" (Luke 2:10; emphasis added). On Christmas Eve, 2004, this angelic pronouncement of two thousand years ago was fulfilled among several hundred Afghan shepherds and villagers in the remote township of Jekdalek, Afghanistan, who on that day heard for the first time the story of Christmas and the "good tidings of great joy."

For several months we American soldiers had visited this village and adopted it as a recipient of humanitarian aid from the families of America to the families of Afghanistan. Due to its remote location in the terrorist-occupied mountains bordering Afghanistan and Pakistan, we traveled by large army Chinook helicopters, which had sufficient room for many pallets of humanitarian aid and dozens of American soldiers to distribute them.

A few days prior to Christmas Eve (December 21, 2004), a team of us made a special visit to the village with the purpose of speaking with the village elders and the local Muslim mullah. Our object was to obtain their permission to return on Christmas Eve to share a Christmas program with their village; the program would include telling the story of Jesus' birth,

Chaplain Allison assists Santa in handing out Christmas gifts to nearly 700 Muslim children.

distributing gifts to their children, and eating food to celebrate the occasion. To prevent an unfortunate international incident, we carefully explained to the village elders and mullah that our intention was not to convert anyone, nor did we wish to cause any offense. We told them December was a special time of year for us, and we desired to share with them part of our culture as they for many months had shared theirs with us. They listened respectfully as I related the story of Christmas as written in the Gospel of Luke. When I finished, I asked them if they had any questions or problems with anything they had just heard. Through our interpreter they unanimously said, "No problem." And then to our surprise the village mullah said through the interpreter: "Christmas is good."

Returning to our base, we prepared hundreds of gift bags for the children, made the necessary arrangements for enough food to feed the village, and recruited interested soldiers to participate. As planned, on Friday (the Islamic Sabbath), Christmas Eve, December 24, 2004, some 230 American soldiers, sailors, airmen, and marines landed via four large army Chinook helicopters at this Muslim village nestled among the rugged mountains and, as promised, we brought food for a Christmas meal and hundreds of gift bags for the children filled with toys, school supplies, and clothing.

Through my interpreter and the use of a handheld megaphone, I requested that all the children of the village (approximately 300) assemble up front to hear the story of Christmas. As the children sat on the dirt in this open-air assembly area, the adults also gathered. It was an interesting sight to behold, with nearly 700 Muslim children and adults directly in front of me and 230 Christian American servicemen standing behind and next to me. Through my interpreter, I addressed the village as follows:

"My name is Mark; I am the 'Christian mullah' for the American soldiers. Our homeland is America, far beyond these mountains, across the desert and over the sea. During the past several months we have learned of your beliefs and experienced your culture and we have become friends. We are grateful to your village elders and the mullah, who have allowed us to come here today to share with you one of our traditions at this time of the year called Christmas. Today we are going to tell you a special story about the birth of a very special child; we will sing songs, distribute gifts to the children, and then eat food together."

Chaplain Allison with his interpreter and the village religious leaders. With the aid of his interpreter, Chaplain Allison blessed the village. When the interpreter told the villagers the American Christian "mullah" was going to pray for them, they instantly dropped to their knees, rifles in hand, to listen to his prayer/blessing for them.

I then pulled from my pocket and placed on my head a bright red Santa cap with its fluffy white ball, which immediately grabbed the attention and prompted giggles among the children. They had never before seen a Santa hat. With their anticipatory eyes and ears focused on me, I began telling them the Christmas story, much as I had done as a father for so many years on Christmas Eve with my daughters Kristi, Hollie, and Ashley when they were little girls.

At the conclusion of the story, I offered a Christmas blessing upon their village. We then, as a choir of American soldiers—Latter-day Saints, Catholics, and Protestants, accompanied by our Sunday worship service organist on a battery-operated keyboard—sang the first verse of seven Christmas carols: "Hark! The Herald Angels Sing," "Joy to the World," "O Come All Ye Faithful," "Silent Night," "Jingle Bells," "Far, Far Away on Judea's Plain," and finally, "We Wish You a Merry Christmas."

At the conclusion of this Christmas program and before Santa's gift distribution to the children, our Afghan hosts wanted to reciprocate by sharing a selection of music and a display of dancing from their tradition. I thought to myself, "Who would have ever thought on this Islamic Sabbath and Christian Christmas Eve that Americans and Afghans, Christians and Muslims would together celebrate in fulfillment of the angelic proclamation of good tidings of great joy regarding the birth of Jesus Christ."

To begin the gift distribution, my commander, Scott Robinson, presented the senior village elder with a gift. This was followed by a Christmas gift from me as the Christian chaplain to the Muslim mullah, which included a hand-held radio I knew he needed for his mosque and school in order to hear news from the outside world. To our surprise, they gave us gifts in return. What an experience! Christians and Muslims exchanging Christmas gifts. Who would have ever imagined it! With all 230 soldiers deputized as Santa's special elves, gifts were then distributed to all the children, each saying to Santa in broken English as they filed by, "Merry Christmas."

There in that remote and desolate, impoverished and humble Afghan village, where the population is entirely Islamic, the true Christmas spirit was both shared and felt by everyone. Although the villagers were all Muslim, there were no anti-Christmas hecklers or protestors of the use of the name Jesus Christ, no legal briefs filed, no court injunctions rendered to stop this public Christmas program, no "PC police" to disrupt the respectful expression and sharing of diverse religious and cultural traditions.

It was a memory-making experience none of us will likely forget: on this Christmas Eve in 2004 in a remote Afghan village, in fulfillment of the angelic proclamation that "good tidings of great joy . . . shall be to *all people,*" Christians and Muslim brothers and sisters heard the story of Christmas—and together celebrated peace on earth and goodwill toward all men.

NO BAPTISMAL CLOTHING . . . EXCEPT THE CATHOLIC PRIESTS' ROBES

Major Mark L. Allison

U.S. Army Chaplain

Afghanistan, January 2004–April 2005

Dispatched to one of the most remote outposts and most dangerous spots in Afghanistan, I saw the hand of God manifested in a history-making first baptism in this country. Utilizing an improvised wading pool made by U.S. Marines near the flight-line at the Coalition Forces Base at Bagram, and surrounded on all sides by weapons and munitions of war, Alexandro Rangel, a twenty-one-year-old U.S. Marine, entered the waters of baptism and became the first person ever baptized into the Church in Afghanistan.

As I made preparations for this battlefield baptism, and knowing we lacked any white clothing, I spoke up at a meeting of fellow military chaplains and asked if any of them had white clothing I could borrow for a Latter-day Saint baptism. My request was met with awkward silence, until suddenly Father Hubbs, a Roman Catholic priest and army chaplain said, "Yes, I have two white cleric robes you are welcome to use—if you don't mind using Catholic priest robes." Hearing this, another in the room said to the priest, "You don't want to do that. The water will be dirty and will stain your white robes." Father Hubbs retorted, "If that happens it will be for a good cause."

Corporal Alexandro Rangel and Petty Officer Juan Juarez stand in Catholic priests' robes prior to Rangel's baptism.

I will always be grateful to this colleague, priest, and friend for his kindness shown on this occasion to Latter-day Saint military personnel.

On the day of baptism, when Alexandro and Elder Juan Juarez emerged from changing from their desert camouflage uniforms into these brilliant white, long-sleeved, and flowing cleric robes, which covered them from neck to ankles, they looked like two angels. It was a sight to behold. Gathered to observe and participate in this historic and joyful event were a small group of Latter-day Saint servicemen and women—soldiers and sailors, airmen and marines—and likely a much larger unseen angelic group beyond the veil. It was a momentous occasion and a memory-making experience none of us will likely ever forget.

My involvement in this story began in the fall of 2004, while I was stationed at the Coalition Forces Base at Bagram, Afghanistan. There, as the Latter-day Saint army chaplain and priesthood leader for the country of Afghanistan, I received one day a crackling, static-filled telephone call from a marine corps first sergeant calling from his firebase one hundred miles south near Gardez. After I confirmed that I am a LDS chaplain, he told me he was calling me on behalf of one of his young marines, Corporal Alexandro Rangel, who two weeks earlier had made a formal religious request through his chain of command to speak as soon as possible with a Latter-day Saint chaplain, if one could be located in Afghanistan.

The next day Corporal Rangel and I conversed for the first time on the telephone. Thinking he was an LDS serviceman in some sort of trouble and needing my assistance, I was utterly surprised when instead he said, "I want to be baptized, and the sooner the better, so I can begin satisfying the one-year membership requirement to go on a mission when my tour of duty is ended. Can you baptize me?" Anyone who is familiar with missionary work knows this sort of golden opportunity does not often occur even under normal circumstances, let alone at the front lines in a combat zone.

Alexandro had grown up in a largely Latter-day Saint town in southwest Idaho, where he had many LDS friends and wanted to learn more about the Church. However, before receiving all the missionary discussions, he was ordered to deploy to the front lines in the war in Afghanistan. While at his remote firebase he continued his individual gospel study and felt the witness of the Holy Spirit testify to his soul of the truthfulness of the restored gospel. He felt the desire and need to be baptized as soon as possible, coupled with a strong impression that he should serve a mission for the Lord's Church.

Anticipating opposition to his baptism and understanding the need for a

Chaplain Mark Allison

person nearby to fellowship him during the process, I inquired if there were any Latter-day Saints at his small firebase. There was one, a navy corpsman and returned missionary, Petty Officer Juan Pablo Juarez, whom I immediately contacted. He readily accepted the battlefield priesthood assignment to fellowship Brother Rangel and serve as his "gospel battle-buddy." Through the next two months, the three of us were in frequent email contact. With the help of the Lord, we surmounted the opposition that soon surfaced in a variety of ways, from the home front as well as on the battlefront, to dissuade, distract, and discourage Brother Rangel from being baptized. Every attempt to bring him to Bagram to be interviewed and baptized fell through. It became apparent that the only way I was going to be able to interview him for baptism was for me to travel to him. I learned of an army Blackhawk helicopter that was going to his firebase in two days to drop off supplies and personnel, and permission was providentially given for me and my bodyguard to ride on it. We would have two hours on the ground to link up with and interview Alexandro and plan his baptism before the helicopter returned to take us back to home base. I immediately emailed Alexandro, directing him to speak with his first sergeant and inform him that I was coming in two days and to ensure that he was at the firebase and not on patrol. His chain of command accommodated the request; and as the helicopter descended at his remote, small firebase, Alexandro was waiting.

I have had many occasions to conduct baptismal interviews, but never in a combat zone and certainly not under the nearby watchful care of Rambo-appearing, heavily armed bodyguards. A few weeks later, Alexandro and Juan were able to get to the base at Bagram. There, on Monday, November 22, 2004, Alexandro was baptized by his "gospel battle-buddy," Juan. Soon afterward, when Alexandro and Juan had changed back into their desert uniforms, several bearers of the priesthood, all armed with rifles and pistols, gathered close in a circle around Alexandro, and I confirmed him a member of the Church. Then my LDS task-force commander conferred upon him the Aaronic Priesthood. It was a circle of priesthood and love, protection and support—not only by sailors and soldiers, airmen and marines, but also by angels unseen. As a colorful flower emerges from a parched, barren desert, and a beautiful rainbow appears in a darkened sky after a storm, this baptismal experience stands as a testimony of peace amidst war, light amidst darkness, conversion amidst conflict—even in the poorest, remotest, and most dangerous spot in the vineyard.

The
HOME FRONT

A few weeks from now I will be sending a son as a missionary to Brazil and my husband as a soldier to Afghanistan. As a mother of a missionary and the wife of a soldier, I am proud of their willingness to serve God and country. Although I will miss them tremendously, I trust the Lord will bless and comfort them while sustaining us back home. As they serve honorable causes, I place them in His care.

—Colette Fillmore

THE QUINTUPLET MIRACLE

Taunacy Horton

Wife of Staff Sergeant Joshua Michael Horton, U.S. Marines

Iraq, 2004

Living a normal and pleasantly private life in a quiet suburb of Chicago was an ideal start for my young family. However, it would not be long before this would change. We were about to become the nation's favorite leading news story.

Our story began when Josh and I met while he served in the marines and I in the navy. We married and were later sealed in the Washington D.C. Temple. Following his service with the marines, Josh joined the police force and I stayed home to raise our two children. As we continued to build our lives, we felt it was time to expand our little family.

After the events of September 11, 2001, Josh decided to reenlist with the marines, knowing he would likely be deployed. After his enlistment, I received the news that I was pregnant—with more than one child. The marine corps gave special permission for Josh to stay home. However, after much prayer, neither Josh nor I felt he should. We knew that other husbands and fathers were far away in Iraq, and it was their turn to come home. "It was the least I could do to let them come home to their families," Josh said on the ABC News program *Good Morning America*.

With Josh deployed in Iraq, I had to experience my progressing trimesters

Shaleigh and Sean hold their four new siblings.

alone. This unique pregnancy made each of the scheduled prenatal ultrasound visits a déjà vu moment. Each time the ultrasound technician peeked to see how the unborn babies were developing, another unexpected little head seemed to appear. Every time I went to the doctor, another baby, then another, and yet another was discovered. After noticing a fifth child I told the doctor, "I'm not coming back!" With Josh gone, I truly had to walk through every day by faith. That is how I made it through this pregnancy.

The doctors frequently shared with me the bleak survival rates of quintuplet pregnancies. During this time I had to completely trust God, turn it all over to him, and leave it in his hands. I found strength in going to the temple and through a lot of prayers. Knowing of my babies' uncertain future, I treasured every day I was blessed to carry them.

While in the hospital I found strength in an inspirational quote painted on the wall of the hospital's intensive care unit. It said, "From small things great things can happen." These words provided me with significant comfort because they reminded me of the words of Alma, "By small and simple things are great things brought to pass" (Alma 37:6). I needed that scripture. Applying this scripture to my situation empowered me during this challenging time.

When I was only twenty-six weeks pregnant, on October 11, 2004, I delivered three daughters and two sons. Their birth weights ranged from 1 pound, 15 ounces, to 1 pound, 9 ounces. Josh was seriously wounded by mortar fire in Fallujah only five days before the babies' arrival. On October 12, unaware that he was a new father, Josh awoke from a coma in the National Naval Medical Center in Maryland. Due to his severe injuries, he was not able to hold his children for another three weeks. Sadly, he never had the opportunity to hold Addyson Juanita, the only daughter who didn't survive. She passed away on October 30 after contracting an infection.

The pregnancy and delivery of the "Horton Quintuplets" made national headlines. The notoriety received by the quintuplets caused me to refer to my babies as "America's babies." It has been a privilege to share them. With Josh serving our country, good-hearted people from near and far took it upon themselves to serve our family. Members of our ward—home teachers, our bishop, and friends—formed what was affectionately named the "Horton Task Force." Senior ward members became surrogate grandparents to the older two children and cleaned our house every other day. The Primary collected nickels, and the Young Men and Young Women made Christmas decorations and decorated our home. Assignments were given to run errands, handle media attention, and sort the growing number of donations.

Incredible generosity was also displayed by large and small companies. A new, six-bedroom home was customized for our needs and then donated to our family. Home appliances, furniture, and computers filled our home at no cost. The Ford Motor Company stopped by the home to donate a twelve-passenger van. (As a bonus surprise, inside the van were Josh's mother and sisters and my parents!) Our relatives' travel expenses were paid by the ward.

Taunacy and her six children. The quadruplets are nearly two years old.

The cable network A&E aired many of these events during a broadcast titled *At Home with the Brave.*

Further Christlike acts of charity were reminiscent of the parable of the widow's mite. One day as I visited the bank, I was presented with a large bag of handmade blankets. Accompanying the blankets was a simple note explaining their loving origin. It read, "I do not have money, but I have talent, and I have time. I wanted to make these blankets for you."

I consider our quintuplets to be a miracle in more ways than one. Hundreds of people have been united through acts of service that have known no limits. I have witnessed how our babies have blessed the lives of so many. They were sent here all at once for a reason. I am truly humbled to be their mother. I always have been.

As I made the adjustment from a family of four to a family of eight, I received strength from words I carefully inscribed on the wall of the babies' room: "By small and simple things are great things brought to pass."

PRAY FOR HIS SAFETY

Susan Brown Wikle

Wife of Eugene "Gene" J. Wikle, Civilian Mentor to Ministry of Defense and Afghan National Police

Iraq, 2006–

When my husband, Gene, was offered and accepted employment in Iraq in 2004, I knew the Lord would watch over him during his service. And if Gene were to be called back to his heavenly home, I knew that was in the Lord's hands as well. Regardless, I constantly carried a prayer in my heart (or out loud) for Gene's safety and good health. I specifically asked Heavenly Father to send my deceased parents and my husband's deceased parents to be guardian angels over my husband there. Gene has acknowledged their presence with him on occasion.

While Gene served in Iraq, a particularly special spiritual experience came my way on the night of October 14, 2004, as I deeply slept. I was suddenly awakened at three separate times and was strongly admonished in my spiritual ears to pray more fervently for his safety. I felt the presence of the Holy Spirit, and felt that that Spirit was joined by my mother, both speaking to me as I was awakened in the night. In her mortal life, my mother always prayed and taught me to do the same. Therefore, on that particular night I did as I was directed from heaven and tearfully invoked our Heavenly Father's further protection upon my husband. My testimony is that we *do*

During a few weeks of leave from his duties in Afghanistan, Gene and Susan took a vacation to Hawaii.

have a loving Father in Heaven who is mindful of each of His children and who hears our prayers.

After awakening the next morning and receiving one of Gene's daily phone calls, I learned that he had indeed been guarded while I slept and prayed. Due to time zone differences, while I was praying in his behalf at night, he was protected in a very significant way. Here is what he recorded in his journal for October 14, 2004:

> This morning I was at the Iraq Ministry of Defense for a logistics meeting. The meeting began with a memorial service for Colonel Azzam, who was assassinated last week. Colonel Azzam was a retired Iraqi Army colonel who was serving as the civilian director of logistics at the Iraq Ministry of Defense. I had the privilege of knowing and working with Colonel Azzam. He was a dedicated man who was doing his best to help bring peace, security, and democracy to the people of Iraq. He was a true friend and a devoted husband and father. The people of Iraq lost a great man.
>
> An American army chaplain of the Islamic faith gave a prayer in

English and Arabic. A member of Colonel Azzam's family was present. The American contingent then presented the Azzam family with the cash donation that we had collected. Everyone in the room was in tears. The Iraqi Ministry of Defense personnel and the Azzam family thanked the Americans for our support and the donation to the family.

After the meeting I rode the embassy shuttle bus back to the embassy. The bus drives right by the Green Zone Cafe and the International Bazaar. . . . After I arrived at the embassy I walked to the PX [post exchange, which is a store] to purchase phone cards for the IRAQNA cell phones. A local Iraqi vendor sells them at a kiosk next to the PX. If the vendor did not have the phone cards, I would have walked to the bazaar to purchase the cards from a vendor. I was at the PX when the bombs [at the Green Zone Cafe and the International Bazaar] exploded. The PX is about 1,000 yards from the bazaar. The explosions shook the PX. I went outside and saw the large black smoke billowing from the Bazaar. I knew by the sound of the explosions that they were bombs. After you have experienced mortar, rocket, and bombs you recognize the different sounds.

I immediately returned to the embassy, where I spent the next five hours. I know that our Father in Heaven is protecting me. I am grateful that he hears and answers our prayers. I begin and end each day in humble prayer. When I am faced with danger like I was today, I also pray to our Father in Heaven. I am grateful for the protection and comfort that he gives me. I am doing my best to stay safe.

With the death of an Iraqi friend, the almost daily attacks that I have experienced, the separation from family and friends, and the hardships of war, I have come to appreciate all that I have in life. I appreciate all that our Father in Heaven has blessed me with. I am grateful that I have Susan [and] my children. . . . I read stories about men who experienced the ravages of WWII, the Korean War, and the Vietnam War and how it changed their lives forever. I realize now that I am beginning to experience that change as well. My life will never be the same. I have no regrets about serving our country, the citizens of Iraq, and our Father in Heaven. The service has all been worth it.

HIS SERVICE BLESSES OUR FAMILY

Susan Brown Wikle
Wife of Eugene "Gene" J. Wikle, Civilian Mentor to Ministry of Defense and Afghan National Police
Iraq, 2006–

When my husband, Gene, agreed in 2004 to go to Iraq as a U.S. government contractor, the very word *Iraq* struck terror within my heart. To then see him pack his limited belongings, bound for Iraq, sent me into a tailspin of panic. Gene was much braver than I. But shortly thereafter, my initial shock shifted. I began to put absolute faith in the Lord, resolved to trust in him with all my soul. I recognized that my husband first belongs to Him.

Later, Gene was transferred to Afghanistan. There he was called to serve

The Saints gathered at church services in Kabul, Afghanistan, in March 2007. Front row, left to right: Gene Wikle and Elder William Jackson.

193

as an assistant to the Kabul LDS group leader, Gerald Brady. A year later, my husband was called to be the Kabul LDS group leader and shortly thereafter as the senior LDS group leader in Afghanistan also. A few weeks before Gene became senior group leader, it was revealed to me from heaven that he would be called as the next senior LDS group leader in Afghanistan. Somehow, I received that revelation before he did. He felt surprised and humbled when he learned of this call from the Lord.

Although I am slowly going blind because of an inherited condition, and care for our disabled daughter mostly alone, and even though I love Gene and miss him very much, I am humbly grateful and even happy to share him with the Saints in Iraq and Afghanistan. He is in service there to our Lord and Savior, Jesus Christ, and he is in service to our country. We don't know when he will finally come home to Phoenix, but he and I will know it when the Lord tells us it is the right time.

Our family is tremendously blessed by my husband's service. He and other wonderful Saints are literally pioneers and missionaries by example in Iraq and Afghanistan, and they are doing so for the Lord. I am extremely proud of them all, and they all are in my thoughts and in my prayers always.

MY FAMILY WAS BLESSED

First Sergeant David Fillmore
Utah Army National Guard
Iraq, 2003–2004

I was given only a week's notice before my battalion was mobilized to begin a training period prior to being sent to Iraq. After being notified, I was very extremely nervous and agitated. Considering the grim reports of mass destruction in Iraq, I was really worried about going over there, and I just could not get calm. During this time of struggle and uncertainty, I knew I needed a priesthood blessing. My neighbor, Burdell Mulford, is a trusted friend and was ready when I sought a blessing from him. He came to my home and spoke words that provided peace to my troubled soul. I remember he said, "There will be angels in front of you and behind you." He continued by assuring me I would return safely and without harm. I was told that my family and their physical and spiritual needs would be provided for during my absence. Following the blessing, it was amazing how I was filled with a peaceful and calm spirit. These inspired words provided me with an immediate peace before I left and a continued sense of well-being during my tour of duty.

During our few weeks of training at Fort Carson, Colorado, we had a Church service that featured a guest speaker. Although I cannot remember the speaker's name, I will not forget his message or the spirit I felt. He made a promise to all of us soldiers that was predicated upon our keeping the commandments. He did not promise us that we would come home safely, but he did promise that our families would be safe and taken care of during our absence. The Spirit was there, and I knew that what he was promising was true. That brought peace to those in attendance, because the welfare of our families was one of the things we were most concerned about.

This all relates to my spiritual growth while serving. I grew most in Iraq through having faith and relying on Heavenly Father. Being in the military, I like to think that I am a capable person. I can take care of myself and my family in most situations. However, when I am several thousand miles away from my family and they are having a problem, there is nothing I can do. This applies even to little things. When someone was mean to my daughter at school, the best I could do was talk to her on the phone. Even then, our phone conversations were limited to five minutes while others waited nearby for their turn. A phone conversation is not the same as being there. I just wanted to be with my daughter and give her a hug. At times like these I learned to take my burdens to my Father in Heaven. Many times I knelt down and put my trust and faith in him, praying for him to take care of my

David Fillmore, on the left, poses with his fellow soldiers.

family. I used to rely too much on my own abilities, but while I was in Iraq I couldn't do anything. Being forced to put my faith in the Lord and rely on him helped me to grow in ways I would not have otherwise known.

It was truly amazing how my family was indeed blessed while I was gone. My boys were not that old, and yet when things went wrong around the house they figured out how to fix them. They could never get the lawn mower to start until after I left. Soon after I shipped out, our yard's sprinkling system broke, and my wife called a professional to make the repairs. After making the repairs, he learned that I was serving in the war. When he billed my wife he insisted on charging only for the parts. It was amazing how blessed and taken care of my family was while I was gone.

I WAS FORTIFIED

Lieutenant Colonel Marc Van Oene
U.S. Army
Iraq, August 2007–August 2008

I leave for Iraq in a few days and will be gone for one year. Attending church today was understandably very special. I loved it all—singing the hymns and feeling the spirit of my home ward. I was greatly fortified; I really needed it; my cup was spiritually filled today. This was my last day of "normal." So to sit there with my wife and family and look out among my friends and neighbors gave me a good feeling. I am going to carry that feeling with me throughout the upcoming year.

Following sacrament meeting, my son was set apart as president of the teachers quorum. It was a choice experience for me to be present and participate. At the beginning of their meeting, the young men stood and recited Doctrine and Covenants 4, which was immediately followed by the Standard of Truth:

> The Standard of Truth has been erected; no unhallowed hand can stop the work from progressing; persecutions may rage, mobs may combine, armies may assemble, calumny may defame, but the truth of God will go forth boldly, nobly, and independent, till it has penetrated every continent, visited every clime, swept every country, and

sounded in every ear, till the purposes of God shall be accomplished, and the Great Jehovah shall say the work is done (Joseph Smith, *History of the Church*, 4:540).

The powerful message of Doctrine and Covenants 4 and the Standard of Truth had an impact on me. As I was listening to those future missionaries, I thought about how I was embarking on a mission of a different kind. I realized that what I was going to do in the Middle East would someday open those countries up to the gospel. Our efforts are opening up their societies, establishing some kind of democratic

Lieutenant Colonel Marc Van Oene

process, increasing their desire for a better standard of living, allowing women to express their opinions—all of which is creating an atmosphere of greater religious tolerance and the acceptance of new ideas. Eventually one day, down the road, missionaries may go and preach the gospel and Muslims may have the opportunity to convert to the truth without their lives being threatened. What we are doing helps open that up.

HE SHOULD GO

Danielle Cobb

Wife of Colonel James E. Cobb, Arizona Army National Guard

Afghanistan, November 2006–December 2007

In 1991 my husband, Jim, wanted to volunteer for Desert Storm. At that time Jim had been in the national guard for about twenty-two years. With six children at home, several of them teenagers, I did not feel I could handle his being gone, at least voluntarily. In 2002, our country had begun fighting the war on terror, and my husband had a longing to serve and do his part. By this point he was a colonel and not attached to any particular unit. He was, therefore, not subject to being deployed with a group. Rather than directly talk to me about going, he would offer such hints as, "They are asking for volunteers" or "There are openings for my rank." I ignored him because by this point we had quite a few grandchildren and life was good.

By 2005, my husband was close to retirement, and we had twenty grandchildren. He had been in the guard for thirty-eight years, his career was coming to a close, and I figured he would not have to go. I am a dental hygienist, and one day I had a patient in my chair who explained that her son-in-law was leaving for a second tour in Iraq. He had two children at home, one who was handicapped. I thought to myself, *You selfish person! Here is a man with two children and a wife, who has already been gone for a year, and who is going again! What right do I have to keep my husband from going? Maybe if he went, someone wouldn't have to go twice!* I called him at work without delay, and with a heavy heart and tears in my eyes I told him he could go.

Little did I know that as soon as he hung up from me, he went online and applied through the National Guard Bureau volunteer website in Washington, D.C. Several months went by without him receiving his deployment orders. By this point, my mind-set was that he should stay home. But then my husband was notified that his application was approved, and he was being deployed to Afghanistan. Because he was volunteering, I knew he could still turn down the opportunity if I asked him to. I was very worried for his safety, and since all of our children were married, I did not want to be alone.

James and Danielle Cobb

We prayed about it and decided to seek our bishop's counsel. When we got to his office, we had a prayer, and then I asked him very directly, "What do you think we should do?" fully expecting him to ask Jim to stay home.

He looked us in the eyes and said very calmly, "I think he should go."

I think my mouth dropped open. *Are you kidding!* I thought.

He must have seen the shocked look on my face (and my husband's large smile) and said he felt very good about Jim going to Afghanistan. He asked me to share my concerns, and I said immediately that I was concerned that Jim would die. The bishop then referred to the prophets' teachings that if you live righteously, you will not be taken before your time. He indicated

Prior to his deployment, Colonel Cobb had this photograph taken with all of his grandchildren.

that he felt that Afghanistan is where Jim needed to be and that there was work for him to do there.

It was difficult to accept. But I trusted in my bishop's inspiration and determined I was not going to stand in the way of Jim's fulfilling this military mission.

Much good came from my husband's time in Afghanistan. In addition to aiding the war effort, his service brought about many humanitarian projects. His service blessed the lives of many, both those whom he served directly and those back home who supported him. I am certainly among those who have been tremendously blessed by his service. I am surprised at how my testimony has grown. It was something I did not expect, and it came in ways I could not have predicted. I missed him, but because I felt that he was supposed to be there, I didn't fear. I prayed, read my scriptures, went to the temple, put his name on the prayer roll, fulfilled my Church callings, and tried to let others serve me.

I am grateful for the opportunity Jim had to serve our country and the people of Afghanistan. And I will forever be grateful for the unexpected blessing of receiving a stronger testimony of the restored gospel of Jesus Christ.

AN APPROPRIATE TRIBUTE

Lieutenant Colonel Steve D. Petters
U.S. Air Force
Afghanistan, July 2007–February 2008

Like the centurion who believed that he wasn't worthy to have the Savior come to his house to heal his servant, I didn't think that I had much of great significance to add this book. However, on reflection, I've decided to share some thoughts that have been on my mind a great deal lately—thoughts about the women who are left behind when we head off to war. In recording these thoughts I know I'll feel closer to the Spirit, expressing something of the divine. (I know that the women who are called to war could write a similar tribute to the men they leave behind.)

As a convert to the Church (I joined while in college), I have often heard stories of the pioneers and their trek westward toward Zion. Specifically, I remember the stories of the mothers who lost husbands (and children) during this period of deprivation and yet found the inner strength to carry on. As I've been away on this most recent deployment to Afghanistan, I've observed a parallel between those pioneer women and the wives and mothers who now carry on with husbands far away, often in harm's way.

My wife and I have been married for twenty-one years. (We spent the last anniversary apart, a common theme during our eighteen-year military career.) We have six children—ranging from nineteen down to six. Since last

May, when I left, one of our sons graduated from high school and started classes at Brigham Young University; his older brother entered the missionary training center for a mission to Holland. During this same period, there have been countless issues with the house. These range from the humorous (children filling water balloons in the sink but getting so much water in the vanity that the drawers were warped beyond use), to the dangerous (electrical outlets that have sparked for no apparent reason). An average day consists of 0500 seminary wakeups, high school volleyball games, and Church activities until O-dark-thirty. (Since I've been gone we've had one child called as the priests quorum first assistant, one as the Mia Maid class president, and a third as the Beehive class president. When these are combined with two still in Primary, it means that my wife is responsible to take the children to virtually every activity that the ward and stake holds.) Intermingled with the already mentioned are dozens of school projects, hundreds of "mommy can you help me with . . ." requests, well over 275 loads of laundry and 1,000 individual meals, all without the companion who promised they'd share the rest of eternity together. In fact, because her spouse wears an air force uniform, Susan has to endure all of the above without the usual help of teenagers who can drive (our last assignment was in England so none of the teenagers could get their licenses), in a relatively new community (we moved to Virginia less than nine

Steve and Susan Petters. Prior to ending his Afghanistan deployment, Lieutenant Colonel Petters was awarded the Bronze Star.

months before this deployment), without the support of family (all Susan's live in Utah—I don't think her parents ever truly forgave me from stealing their baby away from Zion), while working as a piano teacher to supplement our modest military income and taking classes at night to get her teaching certificate.

Truly the same spirit that drove those women across the plains is alive and well in the military spouses of members of the Lord's Church. The burdens are enormous—think of what the Lord asks of families—and to do it all without your partner present is amazing. Of course, there still is a partner, so there are goodie boxes to mail and restless nights to spend wondering if he is safe. And there is worry when an expected phone call from the other side of the world doesn't come: is it only a bad connection? or is it a chance that your loved one has been called on a more permanent mission to the other side of the veil?

I could go on, but frankly I'm ashamed at how inadequate this sounds when I review what I've written. I'm reminded of Alma yearning, "O that I were an angel," or Moroni worrying that the scriptures will suffer for his earthly weaknesses (see Alma 29:1; Ether 12:23–29). I simply can't find the right combination of words to declare the level of devotion, love, and service these women share every moment of every day. Frankly, I'm not sure, given the earthly limits of our communication abilities, that there even are words to describe what these women do and who they are. From time to time I'll hear a new story of the pioneers and their sacrifice, a story that seems so incredible that I'll think to myself that surely it has been embellished—surely no one has that much intestinal fortitude, that much faith, that much devotion. Then, in the quiet moments when I'm in my quarters for the night, I see in my mind's eye my wife, exhausted, reaching for an alarm clock at 5:00 A.M. because she wants to make breakfast for our oldest before she wanders off to early-morning seminary, faced with a to-do list that will occupy virtually every waking moment of her day, serving our children who will not know, and by the grace of God will never have to know, that so many wake up without a mother to love them in this way, and I know in my soul that Susan has suffered far more than I for this time apart. And while I've missed at some point during my career too many holidays and birthdays, missionary farewells, and college orientations my family has had, my sacrifice pales next to hers. In fact, it is only when I look into the eyes of my Savior that I'll ever know a greater sacrifice than my wife has given to me, our children, our nation, and our God over the last eighteen years.

IN SERVICE OF OTHERS

J. Stephen Curtis
**Father of Private First Class Riley Curtis,
Utah Army National Guard**
Iraq, June 2007–

A recent experience caused me to reflect on how hard it must be for our Father in Heaven to part with his children as they leave for their sojourn on earth. The setting was the army's deployment of Utah's 145th Field Artillery Regiment to Iraq. It was an early June morning and emotions were high. A small community had taken time to rally support for a battalion of heroes and give them a resounding good-bye before they headed to war. With sirens blaring, red lights flashing, and yellow ribbons tied to automobile antennas, state troopers, fire departments, police officers, and sheriff's personnel escorted a convoy of vehicles through the town and led our soldiers to the county line. From there, families followed the bus to the Salt Lake Air Base, where they joined others from throughout the state to wish our troops well.

When we arrived at the hangar that would house a farewell ceremony, our mood was somber yet patriotic. Small children waving miniature American flags helped express the truth that freedom is the sure possession of those alone that have the courage to defend it. Leaders of these brave men and women admonished their troops to perform at their highest level of competence, to be the best they possibly could be. Concluding remarks were given

Private First Class Riley Curtis

by the adjutant general, whose words of admiration and encouragement were highlighted with a biblical passage. He paraphrased the writings of Isaiah and expressed his high regard of those he commanded, who were answering a call to duty. Referring to Isaiah 6:8 he stated, "Whom shall be sent, and who will go for us? Then was said, Here am I; send me." The divisions of battalions were then called into formation and separated from their loved ones, part of the final preparations for them to board the awaiting airplanes.

I reflected on the fact that these uniformed patriots who were falling into line as American soldiers were also becoming ambassadors of hope for a war-torn country. One of them was my oldest son, and I was proud of him. Tears welled in my eyes as I thought about the boy who was now a man. This was the child that I would casually refer to with a special call, a summons that would always put a smile on his face and acknowledge a bond we shared together. Standing in the large crowd of onlookers, I was hit with the urge to repeat that call and reconfirm our closeness. So, without hesitation or reservation, I yelled in the same rhythmic tone as I had in years past, "JOHNNY, MY BOY!"—and just as in his younger days, he perked up, looking for his dad. When he finally found me, making eye contact, he simply nodded, and I reciprocated, reestablishing our manly union.

A breaching of the well then occurred, and I began to cry. That signal not only reaffirmed the love between the two of us—just like the union we must have had with our Father in Heaven—but it also conveyed love for our country. It encompassed the freedoms we enjoy that can be related to the plan we chose in the war in heaven. It reminded me that his decision to help defend against a global threat to basic liberties was something he felt strongly about, and that that decision was similar to our decision to offset the challenges of the adversary during our turn on earth.

My son's service is typical of the hundreds of thousands of others who serve in the military and the millions who have served before them. They have thought more about the preservation of liberty than they have about their own lives (see Alma 56:47). We live in the land of the free because of the brave individuals who yearn to preserve for posterity the unalienable rights that have been endowed to all of us by our Creator (see Declaration of Independence).

Freedom has a price though, and it includes requirements that aren't found on the battlefront. Christlike attributes need to be applied daily by neighbors and friends committed to helping the spouses of those who are in harm's way by mowing their lawn, watching their children while they take a well-deserved break, or simply caring and being there when needed.

It can only be imagined how our experience at the hangar might have paralleled what we felt when we left our Father's presence in heaven. The pain and anguish of separation, coupled with the vagueness and uncertainty of how challenges would be conquered, undoubtedly was immense. Yet a channel of personal communication, along with help from a modern-day prophet, has been given to supply needed guidance and direction. Mormon alluded to this in a letter to his son, Moroni, when he shared the love of a father by writing, "I am mindful of you always in my prayers, continually praying unto God the Father in the name of his Holy Child, Jesus, that he, through his infinite goodness and grace, will keep you through the endurance of faith on his name to the end" (Moroni 8:3).

And we can conceive of our ultimate reunion with our Father, which can be described only as incomprehensible joy. Then, through an embrace, we will hear the words, "Well done, my good and faithful servant" (see Matthew 25:21). Welcome home!

SUPPORTING OUR SON

Michael Haller

Father of Corporal Loren Haller, U.S. Army
Iraq, March 2004–March 2005

In a story discussed in Martha Raddatz's book *The Long Road Home: A Story of War and Family*, the reader becomes intimately involved in the lives of some of the soldiers of the First Cavalry Division during a mission they conducted in Sadr City, Iraq, on Sunday, April 4, 2004. It was a day that became known as Black Sunday. On that particular weekend, more than ten thousand miles away, in Anchorage, Alaska, my wife and I were attending a series of televised sessions of the Church's general conference at our stake center.

I recall that a melancholy feeling overcame Sister Haller and me that Sunday morning—though we were unable to understand why. As the day went on, our concern increasingly became focused on our eldest son, Loren. Eager to serve in the war, he transferred from his Alaska national guard unit into the active army's much-honored and much-decorated First Cavalry Division at Fort Hood, Texas.

When he briefly visited home a few months earlier, I gave him a father's priesthood blessing. The Spirit drenched us as the Lord blessed him with safety and a sense of peace and well-being in the face of coming great adversity. It was a moment of sublime clarity—we didn't understand the specificity of the blessing itself, but we unconditionally trusted its Author.

Loren is positioned at the vulnerable top-gunner position as his truck evacuates down a street in Sadr City.

After arriving home from the final conference session that April, we received news of a battle and heavy fighting in Sadr City that involved elements of the First Cavalry Division. It completely captured my attention. Unable to find any real news updates, my wife and I could only wait. Within a few hours of the battle's end, Loren called. He was safe—but his best friend, Dusty, a former Alabama Army National Guardsman with a young family, wasn't.

Loren's loss was deep. A news agency caught video and photos of the engagement. Among them was a photo of Loren defending his fellow soldiers. He was standing in the turret of an inadequately armored, unprotected truck, doing his best to return fire to the enemy. Though he was left with many questions about why he was blessed to survive when others died, he credited the outcome to his father's priesthood blessing and his own Boy Scout training in marksmanship.

We acknowledged that parents have varying levels of worry—and asked him to help us know which level we should have. In the months that followed, we developed a code for our conversations. He'd indicate a level of concern that we could be "allowed" to have. Our code was simple. I would ask, "Loren, are you going on a hunting trip?" He'd respond with, "Yeah, Pop," or "Not tonight, Pop."

Along the way, we had other interesting and reflective conversations. One clear night, when it was midnight in Iraq, he and his patrol were pulled up outside the Martyrs' Monument in Baghdad. The engines in their Bradleys were off. They were set up to intercept the enemy should they come that way. As we spoke on the phone, he began to describe the beautiful mosaic of the heavens above their heads in the night-cooled desert sky. It was a profoundly spiritual discussion—him outside the darkened monument, laying a trap for an unseen enemy, me at my desk in the Anchorage Armory, half a world away.

As we continued our uplifting conversation, the first rounds of the engagement began. In a typical modern-warrior way, he quickly said, "Hey, Pop, I gotta go; the hunting's getting real busy right now. Call you back in awhile." He put the phone down, but hadn't turned it off! I couldn't turn away from the sound of this fractious deadly engagement. It was an unexpected and astonishing moment. I could hear the Bradleys maneuvering and their main guns firing. I heard mortars and machine guns, small-arms bursts and distant explosions. I kept hoping the battle would end quickly, with the Gadianton remnant fleeing before them. It was a profound experience for a parent to share with an adult child. Prayers floated quickly from my lips. Within minutes, the enemy did disengage and retreat.

The Haller family has a legacy of patriotic and honorable military service. Left to right: Logan, Ryan, Michael, and Loren.

Pondering his battles, Loren mourns for comrades that have died and has concern for those who were severely wounded. He has told me that he knows he was spared their particular fate because Heavenly Father still has other work for him to complete. He leaves for Iraq again this October, this time as a leader of troops. He struggles with his Church activity, though he's never stopped believing in Heavenly Father or knowing that the Church is led by a prophet of God. There are no simple answers. With prayer, work, and especially compassion, he and so many like him can and will return.

THE WARD MADE IT BEARABLE

Amy Gabbitas

Wife of Lieutenant Rick Gabbitas, U.S. Navy

Afghanistan

As my husband Rick serves in Afghanistan, each of our four children (Kathleen, age nine; Bob, six; Belle, two; and Tom, one) has learned to deal with the absence of his or her father in different ways. With Rick far from home, we've developed new ways to remain close as a family. A bulletin board near the kids' rooms features pictures, letters, maps, and news articles about Afghanistan. Rick's weekly emails are always featured on the board. Before he left, the kids and I decorated envelopes, with each child having his or her own designated color. When Rick sends them letters, he uses these special envelopes so they immediately know which letter is theirs. Belle doesn't read, but she does know that yellow envelopes mean she has received a letter from her daddy. She sleeps with those letters.

Sundays are the hardest day because that's when we miss him the most. Attending church with four small children is hard enough with two parents, and with one parent it's nearly impossible. I remember one Sunday when Belle threw a tantrum in the foyer before sacrament meeting even started. I just went home. Rick happened to be online at the time, so we were able to chat online. He was having a hard time too, because he was the only Latter-day Saint for at least a hundred miles. We made a deal that I would go to

Belle holding a letter from her dad. The color of her letters is yellow, just like the dress worn by the Disney character, Princess Belle.

church each week, and he would have his own sacrament service each week.

I prayed hard that week that things would get better and that I would start enjoying church again. That's when I received a phone call from a sister in my ward. She simply asked what she could do to help me on Sundays. She and others began to assist me during our Sunday meetings, which has allowed me to be spiritually renewed for another week of being both mother and father.

Our ward has helped out in many other ways as well. The Young Men came at the beginning of the summer and prepared my yard for planting. The Young Women provided baby-sitting. One of the most gracious and unexpected blessings came when an anonymous member of the ward hired a girl to help me twenty hours a week. That is one service I would love to give to someone else someday. This sweet gift enabled me to focus on being a mom instead of feeling overwhelmed. One Sunday a brother in our ward helped me by scooping up a screaming Belle while I was carrying Tom out to the foyer during sacrament meeting. I had never even talked to him before. This kind man then said that he heard I was having car problems and offered to come look at it for me. When he did, he had the problem fixed in twenty minutes.

These are examples of our temporal needs being met, but our spiritual ones are also being fed. We are blessed with a wonderful bishop who has given me blessings and has ensured that my Church callings aren't overly taxing. I have also received many kind comments and inquiries as to how my husband is doing. They have written and emailed him, which I know he appreciates.

Going into this separation, we both knew it would be difficult, and it has been. We also knew it would provide growing opportunities for everyone in our family. I know each of us has gained more compassion for others as they endure their trials. I'm more grateful for the kindness of others, like the nurse who helped me load all the children into the car when we were all diagnosed with pneumonia. We also appreciate our father and husband more than we ever did before. I am most grateful for how this struggle has strengthened my testimony. I've had to rely on prayer to get me through the really tough times. I know my husband has had similar experiences.

Rick and his four children (Kathleen, Bob, Belle, and Tom) at his graduation from training at Fort Riley, Kansas

We're grateful for the gospel and our membership in such a wonderful church. We're grateful for all of the prayers of others in our behalf. As one of my nonmember military friends put it, "You're lucky you're a Mormon because you'll have help and friends wherever you go." That has proven to be the case many times, and I'm sure it will be true for our future adventures in the navy.

A CONGREGATION OF ONE

Lieutenant Rick Gabbitas
U.S. Navy
Afghanistan

Rick and the padre of "The Church of the Resurrection"

My first Sunday during my overseas tour was spent in Kuwait. I was there waiting to take a flight into Afghanistan. I saw that LDS services were at 1400 at the base chapel, but when I arrived the chapel was empty. Two other brethren eventually showed up, both of whom were also en route to Afghanistan. The three of us searched through the chapel and found a cabinet with hymnbooks, CDs, some manuals, and sacrament trays. With a white handkerchief and a slice of bread, we had an uplifting impromptu sacrament service.

After finally arriving at my assigned location, FOB Tombstone, I learned I was the only LDS member on

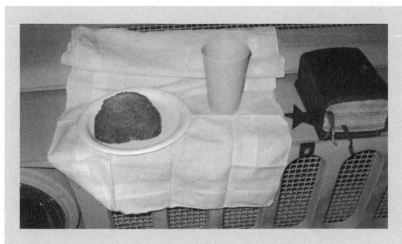

Sacrament service on the hood of a Humvee

camp and the surrounding area. Although Sundays on the base were just like any other day, I still enjoyed worshipping on the same day and near the same time my family was going to church back home. I often attended Anglican services and afterwards I made an effort to find a spot in the motor pool or some other secluded area of the camp to sing a few hymns and bless and partake of the sacrament. As I blessed and partook of the sacrament by myself, I never quite got used to saying "we ask thee" and "all those." I tried to stay on schedule with the rest of the Church by reading the weekly Sunday School lesson material online.

I can be somewhat of a cynic at times. I remember attending church in my home ward and hearing people mention not being able to attend church for a week—and expressing their deep gratitude to be back. My initial thought usually was, "Oh, come on, it's just one week!" I now feel differently. I know how important the congregational experience is. I love singing, and there's really no substitute for getting together with the Saints and singing the hymns of the Restoration. My experience in worshipping as a congregation of one has strengthened my testimony today and will make me more deeply appreciate being among the Saints when I return home.

INDEX OF CONTRIBUTORS

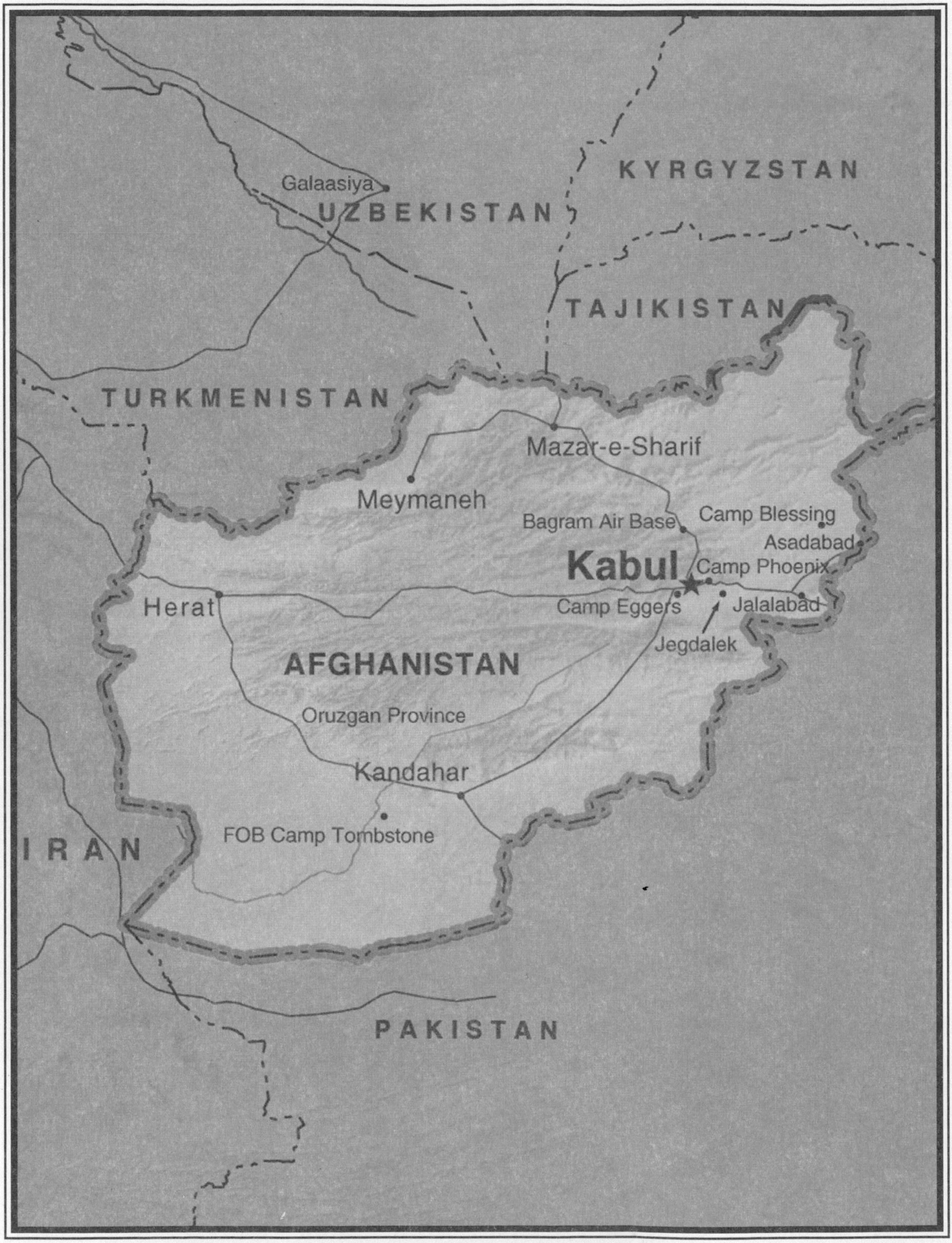
KYRGYZSTAN
Galaasiya
UZBEKISTAN
TAJIKISTAN
TURKMENISTAN
Mazar-e-Sharif
Meymaneh
Bagram Air Base
Camp Blessing
Asadabad
Kabul
Camp Phoenix
Herat
Camp Eggers
Jalalabad
Jegdalek
AFGHANISTAN
Oruzgan Province
Kandahar
FOB Camp Tombstone
IRAN
PAKISTAN